LIVING
WIT
DEERHOUNDS

by

KAY BARRET

Published by Kay Barret 1998

ISBN 0 9533923 0 9

Printed By Upjohn & Bottomley (Ptrs) Ltd., Littleborough

Dedicated to all the Stranwith Deerhounds
over the years
who have asked so little and given so much.

The author with Reason

PREFACE

This book is essentially a collection of information that I have gleaned during my years of living with Deerhounds, from a variety of sources, and from many people, some no longer with us but never forgotten.

It was not written because I profess to know more than others. I realise many are more knowledgeable but may not have the time to put their thoughts down on paper. It came about after a number of (mostly) newcomers to the breed expressed a desire for a modern book, or simply something else to read.

One of my favourite sayings is that when someone has been in a breed for two years they know everything, and when they have been in it for five years they know nothing. I can remember both these stages and many more beyond, during my twenty-odd years in the breed, with all the accompanying triumph and despair. The more I learn, the more I realise there is to know. So with this in mind, I hope that even the most experienced will find something of interest, even if it is just how not to do things!

Much of life with dogs is common sense so I apologise to those who think I am stating the obvious in various sections. Some of you may disagree with things contained in the book and, no doubt, I may also revise my opinions on certain topics in the future, as life in dogs is a process of learning. I would, therefore, welcome opinions and suggestions that could be included in any revised editions. I have tended to err on the side of caution, stating what I believe to be the most acceptable ways of dealing with the various subjects.

Most of the long-standing kennels in the breed have contributed pictures of the best hound they have bred over the years, which should be of interest to both breeders and those new to the breed.

I would like to thank Sue for checking the chapter on health, Tess for nagging, Peter for the loan of his computer and all the people who have taught me so much over the years.

I hope the book will encourage others in their love of the breed, and in sharing the experiences that these wonderful hounds bring us over the years. I wish all of you many happy years of living with Deerhounds.

Kay Barret

CONTENTS

PREFACE

Chapter One

INTRODUCTION TO THE BREED

There are some excellent books about Deerhounds of the past, written by those who had first-hand knowledge of their breeding and of their working ability against their original quarry. It is intended, therefore, to give only a brief outline, which it is helpful to keep in mind when reading the standard.

As early as the third century, dogs of the greyhound type were known and used for hunting. In the fifteenth century, references to and pictures of the English Greyhound, Highland Deerhound and Irish Wolfhound show that these breeds were developing along similar lines and had a marked resemblance to each other. There are various references to the ancestors of the breed as Scotch Greyhounds, Rough Greyhounds, Scottish Deerhounds, Irish Greyhounds and Highland Deerhounds, and it is not clear when they first became known as Deerhounds.

Before the middle of the eighteenth century, there was considerable diversity in appearance, but by then there were two distinct strains, the Highland and the Lowland. The former was taller, stronger and with a heavier coat than the latter.

Originally they were used to course the deer from start to finish. On sighting the quarry, two hounds were slipped to course the deer and either kill it or bring it to bay until the hunters arrived. Later, with the improvement in firearms, they were usually required to track or follow a wounded animal and bring it to bay.

One of the most precarious times in the breed's history seems to have been at the beginning of the nineteenth century, when many of the large Scottish estates were split into smaller estates for sporting purposes, and few then kept Deerhounds for hunting deer. The new fashion was for stalking and shooting, which required only a tracking dog to follow the line of a wounded animal, and for which purpose a collie or similar breed was found to be more suitable, being more biddable and with better scenting abilities. Although a few estates still employed Deerhounds for their original work, on most estates they became obsolete and the breed was left in the hands of a few enthusiasts. Vitality was low and various outcrosses were used to improve size and vigour. One of the most famous 'Deerhounds', Sir Walter Scott's Maida, was actually sired by a Pyrenean out of a Deerhound bitch. He had a lot of white in his coat, but improved size and substance in his offspring. Bloodhounds were sometimes used to improve scenting ability for tracking wounded game and Borzoi to improve quality and grace of movement.

The oldest known strain is possibly the Chesthill, established by Menzies at the beginning of the nineteenth century. Others are Morrison of Glenelg, M'neil of Colonsay and Bateson of Cambusmere. The last provided the inspiration for much of Landseer's work as he considered them the finest examples he had seen.

Towards the end of the nineteenth century, Captain Graham compiled a book of pedigrees of the most notable dogs with measurements and comments on each. It is interesting to note that the average height for a bitch was then twenty-six inches and for a dog twenty-nine inches, (often with a girth of three to four inches more than this), and a height of twenty-nine inches was considered the most suitable size for deer coursing. Although weight and strength were needed, it was felt that a dog much taller than this could be too large and awkward for the job. Agility and stamina were also necessary and, perhaps most important, the keenness and tenacity to pursue the quarry.

The Deerhound Club was formed in 1886 and, when the breed standard was first drawn up in 1892, the height of dogs was twenty-eight to thirty inches, or 'even more if there is to be symmetry without coarseness which, however, is rare', and the height given for bitches was twenty-six inches upwards, with 'no objection being made to a bitch being large unless coarse, as even at her greatest height she does not approach that of the dog, and therefore could not be too big for work, as over-big dogs are.'

In 1907, among the qualities aimed for were a height of less than thirty inches and weight not greater than 105 pounds, with too great a heaviness of bone to be avoided. In 1948 the Standard was amended to the present height requirements.

In the nineteenth century, the advent of dog shows brought change, and sometimes exaggeration, to many breeds but helped to stabilise the Deerhound and give enthusiasts a purpose to aim for now that the original work was scarce. It gave owners the chance to compare and compete and follow common objectives, which are sometimes lost along with a breed's natural purpose.

Many of the enthusiasts then had been lucky enough to see the breed in its original work and would therefore have this in mind when breeding. These days, few owners have ever witnessed this but, nevertheless, it should always be kept in mind, whether you wish to show, or breed, or course other quarry, or simply enjoy the companionship of this wonderful breed.

For more in-depth reading about the history of the breed, readers could look out for copies of 'Scotch Deerhounds and their Masters' by George Cupples, or 'The Scottish Deerhound' by Weston Bell, which has recently been reprinted.

Chapter Two

THE BREED STANDARD

The breed standard was originally drawn up by people who had a working knowledge of the breed at the time that Deerhounds were used for their original work. To keep as close to the standard as possible is the main requirement of anyone involved in the breed as each part is there to either serve a specific function of work or to indicate breeding that is as pure as possible, with undesirable traits from outcrosses having been removed.

The standard is the single most important thing to learn for anyone who is serious about the breed and it cannot be stressed enough that the beginner should learn it thoroughly and that even the most experienced breeder, exhibitor or judge should take the time to read it regularly.

For anyone wishing to show, a knowledge of the standard is necessary as without knowing the virtues and faults of your hound it is not possible to show him to the best advantage. It is not always possible to see what is a correct Deerhound by looking at Deerhounds in the show-ring as it is certainly possible to have an entire class exhibiting the same fault to a greater or lesser degree. Also from time to time, a fault can become so prevalent that it appears to be the norm. From this it can be seen that it is impossible to judge whether a hound is correct without a prior thorough knowledge of the breed standard.

For anyone wishing to breed a correct Deerhound, then again the same rules apply. Breeders need to know the virtues and faults of their bitch in order to choose a suitable stud-dog or they cannot hope to correct any faults in future generations. We all need to have an ideal in mind, a goal to aim for, otherwise how will we know if we are even coming close? The standard is this ideal. Although it is possible to breed a winner by chance, this does not help in the breeding of future generations, and is no substitute for knowledge and commitment. All breeders should be committed to the breeding of the ideal, albeit their own interpretation of the ideal.

These individual interpretations are what makes breeding and showing so interesting. Without these we would all have the same identical picture, use the same stud-dog, and the same hounds would win at every show. The result would be so boring that nobody would be interested in taking part. Individual preferences also help to keep the breed healthier as different breeders place more emphasis on some aspects than others and use a wide range of stud-dogs.

It is, however, important to understand that all variations must be within the standard. We all have preferences as to colour and size, for example, but coat length is very specific. So that if you find that you have a definite partiality for short coats, large ears or gay tails then the Deerhound is not the breed for you. Any variations must be within the confines of the breed standard.

Each part of the breed standard below is followed, where necessary, by a more detailed explanation. I must emphasise that this is my own interpretation of the standard. The standard I have used is the most recent one drawn up and is reproduced by kind permission of the Kennel Club.

General Appearance

Resembles a rough-coated greyhound of larger size and bone.

Characteristics

The build suggests the unique combination of speed, power and endurance necessary to pull down a stag, but general bearing is one of gentle dignity.

Temperament

Gentle and friendly. Obedient and easy to train because eager to please. Docile and good tempered, never suspicious, aggressive or nervous. Carries himself with quiet dignity.

~ I feel that it is a little misleading to say that a Deerhound is obedient as this could imply the instructed obedience of the working collie, which, I am glad to say, I have never seen in a Deerhound. Nor could we say that they are eager to please. They are easy-going and if the thing you are asking them to do is along the lines they were thinking of anyway, they are more than happy to comply. But they certainly do not like to be instructed and to insist that they do something is not the way to obtain their co-operation. All we can really say is that they are probably the most biddable of the sighthounds.

Head and Skull

Broadest at ears, tapering slightly to eyes, muzzle tapering more decidedly to nose, lips level. Head long, skull flat rather than round, with very slight rise over eyes, with no stop. Skull coated with moderately long hair, softer than rest of coat. Nose slightly aquiline and black. In lighter coloured dogs black muzzle preferred. Good moustache of rather silky hair and some beard.

~ The head should be broadest at the point where the ears *should* be set on, which viewed in profile, is at the top back corner of the skull. The top of the head should be flat and should not appear domed when viewed from either the front or in profile. Please note that there should only be a very slight rise over the eyes and, the old standard says, nothing approaching a stop. A heavy head with a skull which is over-large compared to the muzzle, or a head with too much stop looks coarse and ugly. The old standard also allowed for the nose to be blue on a blue-fawn hound, though this colour is seldom seen today. There should be enough long hair on the muzzle to constitute a good moustache and beard, and the practice of removing this hair, as one sometimes sees these days, is incorrect.

Eyes

Dark. Generally dark brown or hazel. Light eyes undesirable. Moderately full with a soft look in repose, but keen, far-away look when the dog is roused. Rims black.

~ Basically the eye should not be so full as to be protruding, as seen in some of the toy breeds, nor so deeply set as to mar the expression or give rise to problems such as entropion. The expression is one of the most important things and is probably the most difficult to define. It is perfectly possible to see a correct expression in a hound with slightly light eyes, and sometimes difficult to see in a hound with very dark eyes, where the darkness can hide any expression at all. The desirable expression is one where the hound looks one straight in the eye, (a definite characteristic of this breed), and yet is also looking beyond and thinking of more important things!

Ears

Set on high and in repose folded back. In excitement raised above head without losing the fold and in some cases semi-erect. A big thick ear hanging flat to the head or a prick ear most undesirable. Ear soft, glossy and like a mouse's coat to the touch; the smaller the better, no long coat or fringe. Ears black or dark coloured.

~ A tiny ear was prized because it denoted purer breeding. At one time, various outcrosses were used to introduce certain desirable traits concerned with hunting - scenting ability for instance. Scent hounds have large ears to help trap the scent as they quarter the ground, and a Deerhound with large ears would denote that the foreign blood was in a recent ancestor. Apart from that, a large ear is unnecessary in a sighthound, more prone to damage and very unsightly. If the ears are set correctly, at the top of the skull, it follows that as soon as they are raised in excitement, they will be partly above the top of the head. Puppies often carry their ears on top of their head, but for an adult to be able to do this at least shows that the ears are set on high. Too often one sees ears set well down the side of the head and it is easy to see that it would be impossible for such ears to ever fall across the top of the head, or be raised above the head. If set far enough to the back of the skull, they will amost touch when the hound has them tucked back. Most Deerhounds grow some fine silver hairs over the top of the black, which are easily removed, but there should be the correct coat underneath.

Mouth

Jaws strong, with a perfect, regular and complete scissor bite, i.e. the upper teeth closely overlapping lower teeth and set square to the jaws.

~ The jaws would need to be strong in order to hold a stag. In the old standard, the bite was required to be level, which means the teeth meet at the front like pincers. As it is obvious that all Deerhound mouths could not change overnight, I take it that both bites are acceptable in the show-ring. In practice, both bites are common, the scissor-bite being preferable as in older dogs, a level bite causes the lower incisors to wear down. A dog should have forty-two teeth in total, the most frequently absent being the pre-molars, although this is not a common problem in the breed at the time of writing. In general, Deerhounds rarely have mouth faults.

Neck

Very strong with good reach sometimes disguised by mane. Nape of neck very prominent where head is set on, no throatiness.

~ The old standard gave a more detailed and specific description: 'The neck should be long; that is, of the length that befits the Greyhound character of the dog. An over-long neck is not necessary or desirable, for the dog is not required to stoop to his work like a Greyhound, and it must be remembered that the mane, which every good specimen should have, detracts from the apparent length of neck.' It also describes the throat as 'clean cut at the angle and prominent.' In the show ring, a long neck can look more eye-catching, and care must be taken not to aim for this at the expense of knowledge of what is correct. For the same reason, there are some who strip out the mane in order to make the neck appear longer. This demonstrates a lack of knowledge of the standard, which states that the neck should not be over-long, and that every good specimen should have a mane. The nape should be strong and muscular, giving the strength to hold the stag, and should give an apparent arch to the neck, beginning just below the occiput. The prominence of the muscle down the front of the throat also adds strength to the neck. The clean cut angle of the throat comes not from removing the hair, but from lack of loose skin, which would have been more prone to injury in the hunting field.

Forequarters

Shoulders well laid, not too far apart. Loaded and straight shoulders undesirable. Forelegs straight, broad and flat, a good broad forearm and elbow being desirable.

~ It is sometimes imagined that the angle of both the shoulder blade and the upper arm (humerus) should be at 45 degrees from the horizontal but in practice this is unlikely to be seen in sighthounds and an angle of 60 degrees is reasonable, with any greater angulation than this being a bonus. The shoulder blade should slope both forward from the withers and also slightly outward to the point of shoulder. There should not be too much width between the shoulder blades at the top and, when the hound is standing with his head in a natural position, the spine should fit fairly snugly between the two, giving a firm feel, rather than a loose, open, weak sort of construction. However, bear in mind that as the hound lowers his head the top edges of the shoulder blades move closer together, so there does need to be some room for manoeuvre. The bones of the shoulder and upper arm should be long, and the longer they are the greater the angulation and the greater the reach in the front movement. A long upper arm sets the elbow back against the deepest part of the chest giving a stronger construction and tighter movement. A prevalent fault in the breed at the time of writing is a short upper arm, which brings the elbow too far forward to the front of the chest, looking unsightly and giving rise to lack of reach in front movement when viewed in profile and various deviations from the true when viewed from the front. With the elbows set well back, there is a greater capacity for muscling of the chest, increasing the strength and appearance a great deal. The forelegs should be straight from the elbow to the pastern when viewed from either the side or the front. The pasterns, which are not described in the standard, should slope gently when viewed in profile but should not deviate to either side when viewed from the front. A short thick pastern reduces flexibility of movement and the hound often tends to stand over at the knee. Too long a pastern would be too weak to stand up to the rigours of the hounds' original work. The pasterns act as natural shock absorbers and in the gallop, or turning, the stop-pad at the back of the pastern often touches the ground, so that a strong and flexible pastern is very important. The bone of the forelegs should be wider when viewed from the side than from the front and should be strong and dense. The tendency to breed for a lot of bone at the expense of quality is to be avoided as heavy, coarse, rounded bone is weaker and unsightly.

Body

Body and general formation that of a greyhound of larger size and bone. Chest deep rather than broad, not too narrow and flat sided. Loin well arched and drooping to tail. Flat topline undesirable.

~ The ribcage houses many of the important organs of the body and needs to have depth, length and a good spring to give the maximum amount of room for the heart and lungs, in particular, to have room to expand, if they are to function to capacity under stress. For the same reason, the lower part of the ribcage needs to have sufficient length before the belly curves upward, and not cut up from just behind the elbow as is sometimes seen. The topline is a very important part of the construction and, though there are a lot of variations, a correct topline is a rarity. It should consist of a series of curves, beginning with the arch over the nape, easing over the withers, which are not so pronounced as in the Irish Wolfhound, and beginning the arch over the loin from approximately the second or third rib from the end. The highest part of the topline will be roughly over the centre of the loin, which should be long enough to give good flexibility but not so long as to be weak. The topline then falls away gradually over a long, sloping croup to the tail. The body should be of a good length as the Deerhound should be longer than he is tall, but the length must come in the ribcage and not only from the loin. Too short a body would reduce the ability of the hound to cover the ground well when moving or from having the scope to cope with difficult terrain.

Hindquarters

Drooping, broad and powerful, hips set wide apart. Hind legs well bent at stifle, with great length from hip to hock. Bone broad and flat.

~ The hindquarters are one of the most important parts of the construction of any running animal, because they instigate all movement and supply the power. As in the forequarters we need the same quality bone and each bone needs to be of sufficient length to give good angulation. The croup should be of a good length and should be sloping, and the hindquarters should also slope outward from the pelvic bones to the hipbones, basically the larger the framework, the greater the area for the muscles which provide the power. There should be good length and angulation from hip to stifle and from stifle to hock, the former giving greater width across the thigh when viewed in profile. It is important, however, that the angulation in the hindquarters be roughly equal to the angulation in the forequarters or the hound will not be balanced and compensatory faults will occur in movement. The hock needs to be broad. The greater the breadth of this joint, the greater the leverage of the tendons that supply the propulsion that drives the hindquarters. It will also follow that the second thigh will have more width, and therefore more capacity for muscle and strength. The hock should be set low, giving a short rear pastern. (Incidentally, there is no such thing as a short hock - the hock is the joint. The correct term is either a low hock or a short rear pastern).

Feet

Compact and well knuckled. Nails strong.

~ The feet must be tight and well knuckled and are roughly cuboid in shape, rather than round, as in cat feet, or long, as in the case of hare feet. The pads are also shock absorbers and should be thick and well-developed, giving the appearance of the hound walking on little rubber balls. A loose, open foot with shallow pads would be more prone to injury when working, and looks very unsightly. Dark pads are supposedly tougher than pink pads, and the accompanying dark nails tougher than pale ones, which may be another reason that dark feet are preferable. Nails should be short, though should come into contact with the ground when the hound is moving.

Tail

Long, thick at root, tapering, and reaching almost to ground. When standing dropped perfectly straight down or curved. Curved when moving, never lifted above line of back. Well covered with hair; on upper side thick and wiry, on under side longer, and towards end a slight fringe is not objectionable. A curl or ring tail undesirable.

~ The old standard said that the tail should reach to within 1.5 inches of the ground which, with a coat of the correct length, means that it will appear to touch the ground when hanging straight down. The set of the tail is most important. It should be set at the base of a long, sloping croup, approximately level with the hip bones and, if correctly set in this position, cannot be easily carried above the line of the back. A gaily carried tail denotes poor rear conformation, usually a short and shallow croup, and sometimes a flat topline. The hindquarters of such a hound will have insufficient or unbalanced angulation, and would therefore handicap him if doing his original work. From a purely aesthetic point of view, it is a very unattractive fault and spoils the outline of the hound in profile movement. (Excuses can occasionally be made for adolescent males, though a correct tail-set makes it almost impossible for even these to carry their tails really badly). A curl right at the end of an otherwise correct tail is sometimes not very noticeable, particularly in bitches who often carry their tails very low, but a large loop in the tail looks rather unsightly, and both are incorrect if rigid. If flexible, however, it has to be said that it would not prevent the hound using the tail to the full to balance when running and working.

Gait/Movement

Easy, active and true, with a long stride.

~ For ease and activity in movement, a hound must be fit and muscled and must also have good flexibility in his joints. To move truly, a hound needs to be well constructed. The three combined will give a hound that complies with the standard and is a joy to watch. Unfortunately such a hound is not often seen. Sound and true movement should, hopefully, be apparent in all the top winners at any particular time and a fit hound should be reasonably active. It is easy, effortless movement that seems to be the missing component, and this tends to come from well constructed and well muscled hindquarters.

Coat

Shaggy, but not overcoated. Woolly coat unacceptable. The correct coat is thick, close-lying, ragged; harsh or crisp to the touch. Hair on body, neck and quarters harsh and wiry about 7cm (3 ins) to 10cm (4 ins) long; that on the head, breast and belly much softer. A slight hairy fringe on inside of fore and hind legs.

~ The old standard gave a woolly coat as bad rather than unacceptable, and listed it as a fault. In fact, a hound displaying this fault often has exceptionally good hindquarters and would be able to his original work without much of a problem. However they are more difficult to live with, requiring much more grooming and care. Nowadays they are seldom seen in the show-ring. The most common coat fault seen these days is the stripped, or over-trimmed coat. The long, fine hair on the ears removed to show off the black 'mouse' ears, or removal of long hair around the feet is acceptable and most show dogs past the junior stage need to be tidied in this way; but any other tidying, while it is accepted that it takes place, should never be apparent. Coat length is specific, as is the slight fringing on the legs, and it is not possible for the hound to have the true ragged coat if it is over-thinned, or shortened. The Deerhound, while being clean and groomed, should always have a natural, ragged appearance.

Colour

Dark blue-grey, darker and lighter greys or brindles and yellows, sandy-red or red fawns with black points. A white chest, white toes and a slight white tip to stern are permissible but the less white the better, since it is a self-coloured dog. A white blaze on head or white collar unacceptable.

~ I have only bred one puppy that had no white at all, and have only noticed one other hound in the show-ring that was free of white, and I think it fair to say that the vast majority of Deerhounds do have some white. For reasons mentioned earlier, I think it best if they have as little white as possible on their feet, although it can look rather attractive on dark hounds if they have good feet, and would certainly never put me off an otherwise good hound. A white patch on the chest would have no bearing on their capacity to work. I have only seen excessive white, (extending up the leg, or from chest up to under the chin), abroad, and not in this country. This may be due to the fact that the old standard said that an attempt should be made to get rid of white markings, and, in the past, it was more common for responsible breeders to cull large litters, when the smallest, followed by the ones with the most white, were the first to go. It may be that if no attempt is made to reduce the amount of white, it may actually increase, as it is interesting that it is so common when the breed has been pure for so many generations.

Size

Dogs: Minimum desirable height at withers 76cm (30 ins). Weight about 45.5kg (100 lbs).

Bitches: Minimum desirable height at withers 71cm (28 ins). Weight about 36.5kg (80 lbs).

~ When the original standard was drawn up, the minimum height at the withers was 28 ins for dogs and 26 ins for bitches. This was increased in 1948 to the present height. The weight was previously 85 to 105 lbs in dogs and 65 to 80 lbs in bitches. This meant that the largest bitch was never bigger than the smallest dog, and the size difference between the sexes was more marked than in most, if not all, breeds. Recently this has been lost and the tendency is to believe that bigger is better, which is not always the case. However, a bitch at the lower end of the height limit looks small in the show-ring. A larger hound is almost always going to be more eye-catching than a smaller one, which is fine as long as the hound is also balanced, sound and of superior quality. Care is just as important in the size of males as, although a large hound is impressive, too great a size would limit the uphill speed and agility when the hound was employed in his original work, which should always be kept in mind.

Faults

Any departure from the foregoing points should be considered a fault and the seriousness with which the fault should be regarded should be in exact proportion to its degree.

~ The old standard listed the faults:

'Thick ear hanging flat to the head, or heavily coated with long hair. Curl or ring tail. Light eye. Straight back. Cow hocks, weak pasterns, straight stifles, splay feet, woolly coat, loaded and straight shoulders, white markings.'

Note

Male animals should have two apparently normal testicles fully descended into the scrotum.

~ Since the new standards were drawn up, the Kennel Club have changed the rules to allow castrated males to be shown with Kennel Club permission.

To help further in the assessment of the breed there is a list of points in order of importance:

Points of the Deerhound

1. Typical. A Deerhound should resemble a rough coated greyhound of larger size and bone.

2. Movements easy, active and true.

3. As tall as possible consistent with quality.

4. Head - long, level, well balanced, carried high.

5. Body - long, very deep in brisket, well sprung ribs and great breadth across hips.

6. Forelegs - strong and quite straight, with elbows neither in nor out.

7. Thighs - long and muscular, second thighs well muscled, stifles nicely bent.

8. Loins - well arched, and belly well drawn up.

9. Coat - rough and hard, longer and softer beard and brows.

10. Feet - close and compact, with well knuckled toes.

11. Ears - small, with greyhound-like carriage.

12. Eyes - dark, moderately full.

13. Neck - long, well arched, and very strong with prominent nape.

14. Shoulders - clean, set sloping.

15. Chest - very deep, but not too narrow.

16. Tail - long and slightly curved, carried low.

17. Teeth - strong and level. (New standard now specifies scissor-bite).

18. Nails - strong and curved.

The standard and the list of points together, when learned and applied, should convey to the serious Deerhound enthusiast a clear picture of the typical Deerhound. The aim should be to try to ensure that the breed continues as close to the ideal as possible, while keeping in mind the hounds' original work, and also the requirements for their job as our companions. We all see the ideal Deerhound in different ways but should try not to get obsessed with one particular point to the detriment or loss of others. Although we may wish to take a certain virtue to the extreme, it should still fit the standard. Exaggeration is not enhancement. The perfect dog has not yet been born, and is unlikely to be, (at least by natural methods!), but that will never stop us trying.

Ch. Aurora of Ardkinglas bred by Miss A. Noble   (Photo by Cooke)

Ch. Upland Thorne bred by Mrs C. L. Osborn

Ch. Gentom Harvey's Honor bred by Jean & Tom Rhodes

Ch. Kilbourne Ruby bred by Mrs G.M. Peach

Chapter Three

YOUR FIRST DEERHOUND

Your first Deerhound is usually the most special, so take as much time and care as you can in deciding. Before considering buying a Deerhound or, in fact, any breed, it is important to establish what is required of the dog concerned. One of the best ideas is to try to talk to as many people in the breed as possible, to get a balanced view of the behaviour you can expect, particularly the temperament.

The most important thing at this stage is to be honest about the sort of temperament you are looking for and not be swayed solely by the appearance, beautiful as it is. There will obviously be exceptions to all the generalisations I am about to make, but we are talking about the breed as a whole, rather than allowing for individual quirks, or taking into account the influence that various owners may impart.

All hounds can be wilful and, to the uninitiated, may appear stupid when compared to a working breed, for instance. This is far from the case, and is merely a ploy to excuse them from being asked to do silly tricks or to have to do as they are told. Hounds are accustomed to thinking for themselves and can be cunning survivors and opportunists. They will turn a deaf ear to their owners' pleas to return and happily carry on with what they are doing. When exercising a sighthound, it is necessary to be able to spot a moving animal or object before they do if you are not going to have to wait for them to conclude their chase or investigation before they return.

Because of this, the amount of obedience that you can expect should be minimal and in fact, too much insistence on this could be an indication that you may have acquired the wrong breed for you. I like mine to return when called, (well, in a reasonable length of time!), for the sake of both my patience and safety. They seem to find it uncomfortable to sit in an upright position for any length of time, apart from as puppies, because of the shape of their bodies, but I do expect them to lie down when I ask, (eventually). Apart from that, I prefer that they don't steal or jump up but most of them do as youngsters. And that's about it. In fact some don't even do this much!

If it is essential to you that your dog is more obedient than this, then a hound is not the right sort of dog for you. Please don't think I am just saying all this to put you off having a Deerhound, there is just no point in both of you being unhappy for the next ten years or so. Of course, it is possible to teach some Deerhounds to do more, if you get the right one and if you spend many hours imposing your will beyond what is necessary. However, to do so is to lose the essential character of the breed which, above all else, should be treasured.

It should also be mentioned that Deerhounds are not much use as guard-dogs. They are usually quiet, (to have one that barks at strangers is unusual), and rather than attack a burglar they are far more likely to give him a warm welcome. True, their size could act as a deterrent, but their size isn't really apparent when they are curled up fast asleep!

Deerhounds can be so infuriating sometimes because they do have a very strong will and are tenacious in pursuit of something they want. On the other hand, their way of thinking for themselves, (and forgive my sounding so anthropomorphic), makes them almost human at times. One of the first things that ever struck me about Deerhounds was their ability to weigh up the difference between two instructions and to choose the easier option, and the way they often compromise between your wishes and their own. New owners will soon realise that what may at first appear to be insolence or lack of comprehension is merely thinking time while they work out what will be easiest for them. The intelligence they will display (or hide) by working out how to get what they want will put most other dogs to shame.

They will never be constantly under the feet, or gazing fixedly at you from a distance of two inches or bouncing about waiting for instructions. They are self-contained and companionable, happy with their own thoughts, unobtrusive and taking up a surprisingly small amount of room for their size. And if you have read this far, then I may as well mention also that they are quiet and easy to live with, friendly with visitors without being pushy, extremely funny clowns when it suits them and the most soulful and sympathetic of listeners. Really the main problem is that one is rarely enough. They can be addictive and most owners have two or more. But for now let's stick to the first one.

Age

If you have the time to devote to the extra care necessary, then there is no doubt that a young puppy is the best to go for. Most puppies are sold at between ten and twelve weeks of age and should only be sold younger than this, to a new owner, in exceptional circumstances. It is generally recognised that, in most breeds, a puppy will settle much more easily if he is younger than twelve weeks, and I think this is probably true. However, Deerhounds are fairly adaptable and puppies are so happy with the extra attention that they soon learn to accept their new surroundings. The slightly older puppy will also have been well-raised for that little longer and will probably be vaccinated, so that if circumstances dictate that yours is slightly older, don't worry too much. His legs will be longer, however, and he will be that much more difficult to catch!

If you would prefer to miss out the puppy stage, there are sometimes older hounds in need of a good home. The Deerhound Club does not have an official rescue as such, but hounds are re-homed, when necessary, with the help of various members and co-ordinated by the club so that you may be able to find a suitable hound in this way. The advantages are that you will be able to see what the hound looks like as an adult, he may already be house-trained and may be past the chewing stage that most puppies go through. However, unless you know enough about his background, he may have some traits that are undesirable and hard to eradicate.

Sex

This is really a matter of personal preference, but do talk to one or two people in the breed before you decide. If you have other dogs in the household, then the age and sex of these will play a part in the decision and provision would need to be made to separate the two sexes when a bitch came in season. Apart from this, I feel that the only real difference between the two is size. An adult male does take up considerably more room than a small bitch so, if house space is limited, then that may decide for you. People who have other breeds usually assume that a bitch will be more loyal, loving and biddable, because that is true of many other breeds. However, I have not found that to be the case with Deerhounds. The males are almost always more loving, from being tiny puppies, and are more keen to be with their owners. Mine virtually always come immediately they are called, unlike the bitches, and seem to want to please more. Unlike many other breeds, they are not particularly sex-orientated so are not difficlt if separated from bitches in season, and I don't think I have ever heard of one wandering off after a bitch that lived elsewhere. Their main drawback is that they do not take into account wind direction when relieving themselves, which can make for wet and rather smelly hind legs! Of course I do love the girls as well, but they are definitely more wilful and more devious!

How many?

Most owners of Deerhounds have more than one and, as there is no doubt that they look impressive in greater numbers, there is always a temptation for new owners to consider buying a couple. However, even if this is your ultimate intention, it does not mean that you need to buy them at the same time. If this is your first Deerhound, and he will be living in the house, then it is probably wiser to buy one. He will be much easier to house-train as he will concentrate more on what you are saying to him and will also be easier to train in any other way, as he will not have the distraction of a play-mate. Two puppies playing together are far more likely to ignore their owner's calls or instructions. Having just one gives you more time to adjust to the idiosyncrasies of the breed and simply to enjoy your first Deerhound, who will always be the most special.

If you decide later that you would like another one, then a good time would be when the first is about three to four years old, by which time he should have a more mature temperament and can be persuaded to be careful with a new puppy. Certainly before two years old, a hound is too much of a baby himself and will play very rough games with the newcomer and could hurt him unintentionally. In either case supervision is advisable for quite some time. Another consideration is that, if two litter-mates are purchased, they will be quite attached to each other by the time they are ten years old or so, having never been separated, and it can be quite devastating for the one left behind when one of them dies, if there are no other dogs in the household.

If, however, it is intended that the puppy is to live outside away from the family, then it is much kinder if two are purchased, as one would become lonely after being used to the company of his brothers and sisters. Two together will amuse and exercise themselves to a greater degree but will also become more independent of human company. They will also get up to more than twice as much mischief as one puppy!

If the household already has a dog, it may be better to purchase two Deerhounds, as one alone focuses on the other dog for its canine company and, temperament-wise, can become similar to the other breed and not display all the true Deerhound characteristics. Unfortunately he does not have a mirror so thinks he is the other breed, and will often be attracted to similar breeds he sees, while ignoring other Deerhounds.

Where to buy
By far the most sensible way to acquire a Deerhound is through the Deerhound Club, and the secretary will be able to put you in touch with someone who will know which breeders have puppies or are expecting a litter. It is imperative that you buy your puppy from a responsible breeder, who will be able to help and advise you throughout the puppy's life.

Although you may have to wait a little longer, it will be well worth the wait and an extra couple of months is not a lot compared to the lifetime of your hound.

Try not to rush into the purchase. If possible, visit at least a couple of breeders in your area, who are usually only too happy to show you their Deerhounds and have a chat to you, even if they don't have any puppies at the moment. If you have more time, then try to find out if there is a championship show in your area in the not-too-distant future and go along on hound day. In this way you will have the chance to see many different Deerhounds and may decide you have a definite preference for one particular kennel. Talk to as many of the exhibitors as you can, (but not just as they are getting ready to go into the ring), and you may find that you get on well with one particular breeder, who may then invite you to visit and learn more. Try not to be too influenced by which Deerhounds win on the day. This is only one judge's preference, and it does not necessarily mean that the hound you had decided you liked was inferior just because it wasn't placed. Also bear in mind that, as in all walks of life, the people with the best sales patter do not necessarily have the best product and that, in dogs, the saying that 'you get what you pay for' does not apply. Find out the average cost at the time and do not pay a great deal more, or less, unless there is a very good reason. However, if you have decided that you wish to show and have decided to buy an older hound that is already showing promise then of course the price would reflect this.

If you want your Deerhound as a pet, then go with your feelings and buy one from parents you like the look of. If you think you might want to show, then this also applies but do spend much longer in your research before deciding on which one to go for. You may have to wait a little longer to get the type that you want but it will be worth it in the end, especially if you think you may eventually go on to breed your own Deerhounds.

Almost all Deerhounds have lovely temperaments, but some are more outgoing than others, some are quieter, so it is better to see them at home as well as at a show.

Sometimes advice is given to the effect that the puppy you buy should be seen with both parents, however a responsible breeder will have put a lot of thought into which stud dog to use, and in at least eighty per cent of cases this will be a dog owned by someone else, who may live hundreds of miles away. The puppy's mother should always be there, though, and is the closest indication to what your puppy will look like as an adult. Allowances should be made for the fact that she will not be looking her best if she has just had puppies - she will have lost a lot of her undercoat and probably top coat as well where the puppies have scratched and chewed but, as long as the puppies have reached a semi-independent age, she should look healthy and should be pleased to see you and proud to show off her family.

When visiting puppies, it is probably wise not to wear your best clothes, but they should be clean and not have come into contact with other dogs who may carry infection. On no account visit anyone else's dogs, whether they have puppies or not, if you have a dog of your own who is ill in any way. An infection that appears mild in a healthy adult can sometimes prove fatal in the very young or very old.

Unless you already show and have particularly asked if you may have a choice of the puppies, it is usual for the breeder to pick out your puppy for you, usually matching the most suitable temperament to a particular home. If you think you may like to show in the future, then you need to be guided by the breeder, who should have a good idea how the puppies should turn out, relative to each other. It is unlikely that any fault will ever turn into a virtue, (for example, a bad shoulder turn into a good one), so don't expect miracles. However, it is quite likely that virtues can be ruined by not taking enough care in raising the puppy. Many a sound-moving puppy has been spoiled by the wrong sort of exercise during the growing period.

These days many people are used to everything they buy being guaranteed, but please remember it is not quite the same when dealing with a living creature. In fact, my advice would be to be very wary of any breeder who guarantees anything, other than the pedigree of the puppy. In particular, two of the things that most affect the ultimate appearance of the adult Deerhound are the size and the coat, and these two things are probably the most difficult to predict. Any breeder will be able to tell you of litters where the smallest puppy finished up one of the largest and vice versa. The coat varies throughout the hound's life, usually starting off short and dark, hopefully the correct length as a mature adult, but of unpredictable colour, usually lighter than the puppy coat, then becoming heavier and darker again with age. But there are, no doubt, many exceptions to this too.

If you wish to show and/or to breed, buy a puppy from well-bred parents that you like. Third choice bitch from this litter may well be a better prospect for you than first choice from a litter that has been bred haphazardly, and is far more likely to produce the type you want when you go on to breed from her in the future.

When you go to see the puppies, they should appear healthy, and should be happy and outgoing. Of course there will be times when they are asleep, but it usually doesn't take long for them to re-charge their batteries, especially if there is something interesting going on, like the arrival of visitors, so that by the time you have met the adults, (who should also be healthy and happy), and had a coffee, the puppies will be wide awake again. For the journey home, I find that puppies travel best in the footwell in front of the passenger seat, probably because they are wedged in more and can't see things going by, which is less likely to make them feel sick. However, it is best to take a supply of towels, newspapers and kitchen-roll to mop up on the way.

The breeder should give you the puppy's pedigree, showing the ancestors for four or five generations back, which may not mean a lot to you now, but is nice to look at and will be very interesting to you if you decide to show; the Kennel Club registration certificate, (though in many cases this will not have come back from the Kennel Club by the time the puppies are old enough to leave home, so, as long as you are buying from an approved breeder, don't worry); a puppy insurance certificate, which will cover him for the first six weeks in his new home; a certificate to say that he has been tested and is clear of liver shunt; and an information sheet.

The latter should contain details of when the puppy was wormed and hints on future worming, any vaccinations already done, details of how much and how often to feed, instructions on exercise and general information on how to deal with a puppy of a large breed. It should also contain the breeder's telephone number, in case you have any problems. Do keep this safe and, most important, read it! It is somewhat dismaying when purchasers ring up a week later asking a question that was answered on the sheet, if they had only bothered to look!

The breeder will also give you some of the food that the puppy has been eating to date, though it gives a good impression if you have thought to ask in advance what the puppy is eating and have bought a sack in readiness for his arrival. It is important that you feed the same food initially and that any changes are made gradually.

Faults

All puppies, in fact all dogs, have faults, and in most cases they are minor construction faults and will not adversely affect his role as your companion. If you wish to show, then you should ask the breeder's advice and any noticeable faults will be pointed out and discussed. Puppies change all the time and some faults will improve and some will get worse. Different parts of the puppy grow at different times and proportions will change, but should correct themselves so try not to worry.

I have known new puppy owners to be quite concerned about things they view as faults, that are actually virtues. One owner, each time I spoke to her, expressed concern that the baby always had her ears on top of her head instead of carried like my adults, and no amount of reassurance helped, only time. With no other experience of Deerhounds, she was not to know that this meant that the puppy had very well-set ears and she actually should have been pleased. (Besides looking rather cute!).

Owners can even get to like faults. I remember talking to one gentleman I hadn't met before, (at a show!), who was telling me that he was pleased that his new puppy had cow-hocks because their previous Deerhound had them too, and he rather liked them!

Some faults are more of a problem to sort out. A woolly coat should be obvious by the age you collect your puppy, at least to the breeder. It is only one fault, of course, and will not affect the health or fitness of the hound, but unfortunately it does change the entire appearance, so that the Deerhound rather resembles a large Bearded Collie. It is also a lot more work to keep it well-groomed. If you wish to show, there is obviously no point in having this one out of the litter, (however well-constructed it is - and it most probably will be), though it would not matter if the hound were to be just part of the family, and I would expect the puppy to cost considerably less.

A fairly prevalent fault in Deerhounds is one or both testicles not descending. The ones with one testicle are usually called 'monorchids' (though more correctly, 'unilateral cryptorchids) and the ones without any are usually called 'cryptorchids' (bilateral cryptorchids). Unfortunately, it is difficult to know at the time of purchase whether or not the puppy will eventually become entire, as puppies can become entire from six weeks onwards, but the latest I have heard of one becoming entire was at thirteen months. Some breeders will reduce the price of a puppy that is not entire, though if he became entire later it would probably be necessary to pay the difference. To be on the safe side, vets, if asked by puppy owners, advise removing the retained one in case it causes problems later but, though I have asked many people, I have not yet heard of any problems in later life and there are quite a large number of monorchids out there. It is my feeling that it is pointless to entail the risk of a general anaesthetic unless it is for something absolutely necessary. It is as well to note that cryptorchids are not fertile but monorchids are, though should not be bred from as they will pass on this predisposition.

Continuing care

If you have any problems or worries after you take the puppy home, and for the rest of his life, the first person to contact for advice is the breeder. Any responsible breeder will be more than happy to sort out anything you are worrying about. Quite often, you will find that it is something common in the breed, or a usual stage they go through, and that you have nothing to worry about. Usually just talking it over helps. Obviously if it is a matter of life or death, a serious accident for example, then immediate veterinary assistance is necessary, but in other cases it is probably better to talk to the breeder first. Sometimes vets can worry an inexperienced owner more than need be, simply because they are probably talking about dogs as a whole rather than Deerhounds, and they are trying to cover all eventualities. Behavioural problems can also be talked over with the breeder. In all cases, even if they don't know the answer, they should be able to advise you on whom to discuss your problem with.

Even if you don't have any problems, try to contact your breeder occasionally, just to say how wonderful the puppy is, and how pleased you are with him. It is music to any breeder's ears!

Two typical puppies

Chapter Four

PUPPY CARE

Looking after a puppy is a very time-consuming business and you will find it hard to remember just what you had time to do before his arrival. Because of this, if you work full time, it is not a good idea to contemplate having a youngster, (or even an adult unless provision can be made for someone to take him out and keep him company for a reasonable part of every day). If you work part-time, then arrange to pick up the puppy when you can take some holiday, as there is no doubt that the more time you can spend with him at this stage, the easier it will be to get him settled in and used to your ways. Most habits are easier to establish than they are to break.

It is a good idea to have everything ready before you collect your puppy so that his arrival home can go as smoothly as possible. After the journey take him first to the place in your garden that you would like him to use to relieve himself and give him chance to do this, though he will probably be too excited and will want to explore. Apart from showing him the water bowl and his bed, the only things necessary for the rest of the first day are to feed him, as suggested by his breeder, and to take him outside regularly. It is not a good idea to keep calling him to you and fussing him overmuch and children should understand that he is to be allowed to settle in quietly, rather than expecting him to want to play immediately. If allowed to settle in at his own pace, he will soon make it known when he is ready for some attention.

Children

All dogs should respect people and should not ever be allowed to growl, much less snap, without being severely reprimanded. Having said that, there are sometimes mitigating circumstances. Dogs are not toys, and no dog should be expected to allow a child to poke him or pull him around or be generally thoughtless, and even the most loving and careful child can accidentally hurt a dog when playing or falling over. I am still not condoning the dog retaliating in any way. However the best idea is to prevent it happening in the first place.

As well as the puppy being taught to respect the children, the children should also be taught to respect the puppy, (and in fact all animals). In general, I have found that Deerhounds love children. (They are, after all, a very convenient height and often drop tasty food on the floor). However there are times when they like to be left alone, and when they have had enough tend to go out of the way rather than complain. They must be allowed to do this and not followed. They should have somewhere of their own, preferably their own bed, to retreat to that is out of bounds to the children. If this is an accepted rule, then there should never be a problem.

Older dogs
Dogs that are already a part of the household can become very jealous of the newcomer, so if there are more than one should be introduced gradually. Some dogs really don't like puppies but will be all right once the puppy is older. An only dog is more likely to mind the intruder but if they get extra fuss at the same time as the puppy may eventually learn that the puppy is a good thing. It is not a good idea to leave them together unsupervised for quite a long time until you are absolutely sure there is no animosity or that the games will not be too boisterous. Puppies can be easily hurt and the weight of an adult dog of any size hitting him when running can cause irreparable damage. The puppy will often not realise when either he or the other dog has had enough and it will be up to you to intervene.

Bedding
If the puppy is living in the house, the most preferred type of bed seems to be a bean bag, which is a cotton bag filled with polystyrene, or similar, beads. Ultimately he will need the largest size that you can get or, if you are making your own, about a yard or a metre square. There is no doubt that these beds are comfortable and warm and mould to the shape of the dog, as well as keeping him well off the floor and out of draughts. They need to have an outer cover which can be removed for washing. Unfortunately, if the puppy decides to explore the contents of his bed overnight, you will come down in the morning to what looks like a snowstorm and the beads are not very easy to sweep up.

Perhaps at first it is better to use the acrylic fur type of bed, manufactured by various firms and now available in many colours. These are easy to machine wash and quick to dry as well as comfortable for the puppy. They are supposed to be chew-proof, and they do last for quite a while unless the puppies are really determined. A large cardboard box with a piece of this would serve very well for the first few weeks, by which time you may have been able to persuade him to look after his bed. If you stick to this type of bed he will need the largest size available by the time he is a few months old, and preferably double thickness.

If space will allow, a single mattress on a wooden base would give him plenty of room to stretch out. If it is well-covered, then hopefully he will not discover it is very chewable.

If the puppy is to live out in a shed or kennel, with a run, then any of the above would also serve him quite well, though it would be a good idea to contain them in a large wooden box so that they do not get dragged outside when playing. A more usual idea is to fill the box with straw or shredded paper into which the dog can dig himself to keep warm. In the winter it will probably also be necessary to have a heat lamp or a wall-mounted kennel heater, especially if he is living alone. It goes without saying that these must be safe and secure so that the puppy cannot burn himself or chew the wire and so that they cannot be knocked down onto the bed where they will catch fire. Any box should be of sufficient size that the hound will be able to lie down on his side as an adult, with enough room to stretch out his legs.

The first night

For the reasons mentioned earlier I think that the first night the puppy is best left on his own, rather than with any other dogs you may already have, even though the other dog would be company for him. Probably the ideal would be for the puppy to be able to see the older dog but not be able to reach him, though this is not always easy to arrange.

Some people leave the light on so that the puppy can find his way round his unfamiliar surroundings. This may be a good idea the first night but after that it is better to encourage him to get into the habit of sleeping at this time, so the fewer distractions the better.

Unless the room is very cold, there should be no need of a hot-water bottle. In the end he will have to do without it or he would just chew it. Some people wrap up a clock to put in the bed with the puppy, but clocks aren't very comfortable, and I'm sure any puppy can tell the difference between a clock and the heartbeats of his litter-mates! A radio playing quietly may help him to believe he is not alone.

Most puppies cry a little initially, and one of the most difficult things is to harden your heart and ignore him. After his goodnight cuddle he must learn that he is on his own until you reappear in the morning, and the quickest way, and the most painless for him, is for you to ignore his pleas. If you go back to him, it is simply prolonging the agony for him. It is also teaching him that you will go to him when he calls - this is the wrong way round and is establishing bad habits for the future.

If he cries excessively, shout at him through the closed door. Then ignore him! If you have neighbours it may be a good idea to warn them that you are getting a new puppy who may be noisy at first. Hopefully they will be understanding. If you can stick to your guns then it should not take too long. If you keep giving in to the puppy, it will take much longer and be more disruptive to everyone concerned. There are always going to be times when he must be left and it is better that he learns this as soon as possible.

You owe it to him to make every lesson as quick and painless as possible. This is the first lesson that he will learn, and how it is dealt with will establish a pattern for future lessons. The more quickly he learns anything, the more time you have left for those compensatory cuddles!

Feeding

The most important food is water, which should always be available. It must be clean and should be emptied and renewed a few times a day. It is best raised off the floor so that it is at the right height for drinking and the bowl is less likely to get knocked over when the puppy is playing around.

When the puppy arrives, give him a couple of hours, at least, to settle down before you offer him any food as before then he will be too excited to pay it any attention. Follow the breeder's instructions and offer him the amount he is used to, or slightly less. Don't be tempted to give more even if he appears to be asking for some. Again it is better to establish good eating habits at this stage. Over-facing him will lead to his leaving food in his bowl, which is not what you want.

Any type of feeding bowl is suitable, though plastic ones may be played with and chewed. Stainless steel bowls are more expensive but are easy to keep clean and last indefinitely. The bowl should be placed at chest height so that he does not have to stoop to eat, and should be raised as the puppy grows. Eventually, a kitchen chair is about the right height for the bowl and is convenient.

If the puppy does not eat well the first day, it is probably due to excitement, but after that it is time to re-think. If food is left in the bowl, then remove after about ten minutes and throw away - old soaked food is not very appetising later and in warm weather could go off and make the puppy ill. As a breed, Deerhounds are not usually greedy and he will be missing the competition of his litter-mates. At the next meal feed less and, if he finishes it, stick to that amount for a few days to get him used to cleaning out the bowl. If he still doesn't eat, reduce again and continue until you find an amount that he is happy with. Do not encourage him or fuss round him if he doesn't eat, or even hover over him anxiously, as this will make him worse. He will either enjoy the extra attention and play up to it or he will think something is wrong and not eat because he is worried. They are quite in tune with us mentally and can pick up on an owner's anxiety, even if the owner is pretending not to care. There is no need to panic, thinking that this is a large breed and needs to eat a lot. A few days will not matter in the general scheme of things and if you can just treat the whole business in a matter-of-fact way, and again just ignore the puppy's behaviour, he will soon learn that he has a few minutes to eat and that prolonging it will mean he goes hungry and does not get extra attention. Most importantly, please do not be tempted to change his food at this stage, or add extras or tempt him with titbits. All you will be teaching him is to leave various types of food. You are far more likely to create a fussy eater, which will make life far more difficult for you in the future, and will not make him any happier. Again it is just prolonging the agony for the sake of just being a little firmer with him for the first few days. Bear in mind that he has been eating this food happily for the past few weeks and does not know any other, whatever you think he is trying to tell you. And I have never heard of a Deerhound starving himself to death!

If he eats well, praise him. Do not give him any more food at this time. It is best to stick to the amount he has been used to for at least a week. After that, if he is eating every meal eagerly, you can increase the amount very slightly every few days, to appetite. Don't be tempted to overfeed, which may just make the puppy sick or give him diarrhoea.

When you first get your puppy he is likely to be eating four meals per day. This can be reduced to three meals at about four months of age, though obviously the amount at each meal would increase. Three of the meals should gradually be increased as the fourth is reduced. At around six or seven months two meals per day should be enough, again changing over gradually. Most owners feed two meals per day throughout the hound's life as, certainly on some types of food, it is difficult to feed sufficient quantity at one meal without overloading the stomach.

House-training

The first few days are the most important in house-training your new puppy and time invested now will not be wasted. If you spend literally all his waking hours keeping an eye on him, then it should only take a few days for him to learn how to be clean during the day. If you do it half-heartedly, it will take much longer.

If the weather is suitable, by far the easiest way to house-train a puppy is to leave the door open all the time so that he has access to the place you want him to use. Watch him each time he goes out and praise him when he has the right idea.

If it is winter or the weather is poor, then you will have to take him out regularly - every hour at first if possible - so that he never has to wait very long in order to keep his house clean. Most puppies do want to be clean, and given the opportunity will comply. Gradually increase the time interval between going out as long as he realises that if he holds on he will be going out soon. When you take him out for this purpose, walk him round in the place you wish him to go, while encouraging him with whatever word you have decided to use. (Try to choose one which won't be too embarrassing to use in public!).

The times he most needs to go out are first thing in the morning, as early as possible to start with, each time he wakes up, after each meal and last thing at night, as late as you can.

During the night, it will be more difficult for him and you will probably have to be more patient before he will go all night. Some people use newspapers to train puppies, in which case care must be taken not to leave newspapers you still wish to read lying around on the floor!

If he has an accident, as is bound to happen sooner or later, and you catch him at it, a stern 'no' will be enough to stop him in his tracks. Take him outside immediately and praise him when he continues outside. If you find a puddle indoors, there is no point in shouting at the puppy as he will not associate the shouting with the puddle and will just become upset. It is much better to be on your guard to prevent it.

If the puppy or puppies live out in a shed with a run, then leaving the shed door open so that they have constant access to the run will ensure that they learn to use outdoors. In this case you will have them in the house only when you have time to give them your undivided attention, so accidents are less likely to happen.

Chewing

All puppies chew! Deerhounds are not as destructive as some other breeds, and some hardly chew a thing. I find the most difficult things to persuade them not to chew are my hands and clothing, but maybe it is more difficult when they are home-bred and have got into the habit from the time they were too tiny to reprimand.

Deerhounds are sensitive creatures and do not like to be shouted at. They find it more of a punishment than being smacked, so usually a quick 'no' when they are doing wrong will stop them, at least temporarily, although just because they know something is wrong does not always stop them doing it.

From the time you get your puppy until after he has finished teething is a most difficult time for him. It is also unpleasant for you to constantly feel you are telling him 'no' so that it is probably wise to pick a few habits you wish to eradicate, rather than try to stop all of them at once. As usual, prevention is better than cure. Although this seems to be stating the obvious, if you have valuable furniture it is much wiser to move it out of any room in which you are likely to have to leave the puppy unsupervised. It takes no time at all for an active puppy to do extensive damage to a chair leg or a table top, if the fancy takes him. It is far better to remove temptation and watch for any signs of chewing on the furniture that he has access to. When you see the first signs, it is time to keep an eye on that particular corner, or whatever, and watch for the next chewing session. If the puppy persists, it is an idea to spray the area with an unpleasant tasting spray sold for this purpose. Alternatives are nail-biting preventatives or oil of cloves. Another way to prevent access to items that you want to keep intact, if they are all in one area, is to block that area off with wiremesh puppy panels, leaving him free to roam in the rest of the room where damage doesn't matter so much.

Puppies will often chew shoes, (only one out of the pair, though), bags, ornaments, baskets and anything else that looks inviting. It is always the fault of the owner. A dog cannot chew something unless it is within his reach, (and unfortunately they have a much greater reach than many dogs). Having a young dog in the house is like having a toddler and things just have to be kept out of his way for a while, or alternatively he has to be kept out of their way. It goes without saying that any dangerous items like bleach, medicines and so forth should be doubly secure.

If the puppy has your company for most of the time and if he has plenty of time to run in the garden and play, then he is far less likely to get up to mischief. Chewing is more likely to occur when the puppy is bored.

Toys

There are many sorts of toys on the market and it is largely a matter of personal preference which you will buy. Do make sure, though, that you get large sizes of anything, as small chews, balls etc. can get stuck in the throat when the puppy is playing. Mine love their Kong, a toy which bounces erratically, and also like ropes or similar items that they can pull and toss around. Chews that have some food value are probably best left until after you have established good eating habits, but there are bone-shaped toys that just help massage the teeth and gums and give relief to teething puppies. If you do not want to spend a fortune on toys, they can be just as happy with old socks knotted together, empty plastic bottles, (tops removed), cardboard boxes and the like, though more care is needed to make sure the puppy is not actually swallowing bits that he chews off.

Exercise

Enforced exercise is not necessary or desirable until the puppy is around ten months old, and it is actually likely to do damage. Until this time, he just needs a garden or a safe field to play in, where he can run or rest as he chooses. Once he has had all his vaccinations and is deemed safe to go out, then it is possible to start lead-training if this is desired. Walks on the lead should be limited to a hundred yards or so, just to get the puppy used to the lead and to traffic and other people and dogs. It should not be increased much until the puppy is much older and then only very gradually.

It cannot be stressed too strongly how easily damaged are the growth plates in the puppy's limbs. The puppy may look bigger than many other breeds, but he continues to grow, very rapidly, for many months. It is therefore not a good idea for him to get his exercise by running up and down stairs or steps, or jumping on and off the furniture, or anything that causes sudden or undue stress to his legs. I am sure you will be given these instructions by the breeder of your puppy but it does no harm to emphasise them. It may seem a lot of trouble, but by the time you get your puppy, there will only be another seven months or so to go and this is only a fraction out of your puppy's life and will soon pass. If you don't care what he looks like then it doesn't matter too much, but if you might wish to show later on, then the extra care taken now will be worth while. If you must have your Deerhound sleeping in the bedroom with you, his walking upstairs slowly will not do any harm but he should be carried down again in the morning while small, and made to walk slowly downstairs when too heavy to carry. It is the repetitive jolting of his joints that does the most damage.

Stairs can be cordoned off by a child-gate at the bottom and steps in the garden can also be blocked off in some way. Any other hazards should also have a suitable deterrent, and all this should be done before you get the puppy. Anticipation of the puppy's behaviour can prevent many accidents.

Vaccinations

These days there is a lot of controversy about vaccinations, both whether they are necessary and whether they cause more problems than they prevent. Even some vets seem to be questioning whether wide-scale annual vaccination is necessary. It is a personal decision and it is best to read and listen to the current findings on the subject before you make your decision, as new evidence is coming to light all the time.

However don't base your argument on the fact you feel safe because you think that diseases are a thing of the past because you don't hear of them much any more. They have been controlled to this extent because most dogs in most areas are vaccinated. Also just because you live in an isolated area and your hound may be exercised totally on private land, does not mean that other dogs cannot pass by and infect him. A dog leading an isolated life is more at risk because he does not build up antibodies in his system that are produced and topped up by contact with these diseases.

These days some people are using homeopathic preventative measures, though I have no experience of these myself. If you wish to use this method, it is important to take advice from a qualified homeopath who has enough experience of treating animals in this way.

Dogs are usually vaccinated at ten and twelve weeks, though this can vary, against distemper, leptospirosis, hepatitis, parainfluenza and parvovirus. Vets like them to have an annual booster and boarding kennels may also insist on this. Some kennels also insist on a vaccination against kennel cough.

Worming
The puppy will probably have been wormed three times by the time he is ten weeks old, with one of a variety of preparations available from the vet. Regardless of whether you have noticed any worms or not, the puppy needs to be wormed again at four to six months of age and then again every six months, using a wormer obtained from your vet rather than one bought over the counter at a pet-shop.

Grooming
At first the puppy will have little coat and needs only a soft bristle brush, just to get him used to the experience. Most will learn to enjoy it if you make it a pleasurable time. As he grows a coat then a padded brush with metal teeth with bobbles on the end, does not hurt and will go through the coat more easily. From the beginning it is a good idea to get the puppy used to having his feet and nails handled. At this stage the nails are quite soft and he will probably keep them short by playing in the garden and scratching at things, but eventually you will have to trim them at times, so get him used to the noise or feel of the clippers.

Leaving the puppy alone
No matter how much time is spent with the puppy, there will be times when he will have to be left alone and it is as well that he gets used to this. After he has had a week or two to settle in and feel secure, leave him for very short periods. This can be increased gradually up to a couple of hours, picking a time when he will not need to go outside. Making a big fuss about leaving him will make the puppy think there is something wrong, so try to be matter-of-fact about it and save the cuddles for when you return. If you pick a time when he is likely to sleep, he may not even miss you!

Ch. Ardneish Scourie bred by Betina Adams

Ch. Almondbank Ardua bred by McIntyre & Nicolson

From puppy.......

....to Champion Dufault Palladium bred by Miss C.P. Cox

Chapter Five

PUPPY TO ADULT

Once the puppy has settled in, there begins the most important period in his life with you, when the adult hound gradually emerges, albeit through some rather strange-looking phases. In this period he will establish eating and other habits, and develop his character through trial and error. At this time owners will both derive the most amusement and also suffer the most anguish if they do not tackle any problems in the right way.

Around the house

If there are to be any no-go areas in the house, these need to be established right away. It is no good letting the puppy go anywhere he wants to start with, because he's cute and the family want him around, then expecting him to understand when he is banned from an area. Consistency is the most important part of any training and the family must present a united front. If you have decided to allow him on the furniture, it may be better to give him a sofa of his own that can be covered with a sheet for ease of washing. Not all visitors appreciate getting a film of grey hairs on their clothes when visiting you. But then, it can be quite a good method of avoiding unwanted visitors. Regular callers must learn to deal with an affectionate grey lump draped around their shoulders.

All puppies have times when they enjoy a mad half-hour, but the chosen race-track should be made as safe as possible. It should not include stairs, steps or furniture as bouncing on and off these repeatedly will damage his growing legs. For the same reason, skidding on mats on slippery surfaces is not to be encouraged and has caused many a broken leg. They do find it such fun, though.

He may still do this occasionally as an adult, when it will be even more amusing, but in general the adult hound is rather lazy. Give him a comfortable bed and you may not see him for hours at a time, unless you start to prepare his favourite meal, or it is time for his walk. Even the walk may not be appreciated if it is raining, though it will be tolerated as long as you are getting wet as well. If you are expecting him to go out in the garden to get wet on his own, it is a different matter and you may need all your strength to push him outside. Snow is a different matter and this is welcomed as great fun, at least the first few times each winter. If it is deep, he will get snowballs all over his legs, which will need to be combed off when he comes in. The snow also collects in tight balls between the pads and can be quite uncomfortable. If walking in snow, these need to be removed regularly.

Socialising

Deerhounds are usually friendly and laid-back, and the need for socialising isn't as necessary as for some other breeds. Hounds living in towns will get used to the sight and sound of people, traffic and other dogs, and will soon learn to take everything in their stride. For those living in the country, who may see only their owner, it will not do any harm as long as it is undertaken with care.

Once the puppy's vaccinations have taken effect, and he is used to walking on a lead, he could be introduced to training classes, if so desired. When he is over six months old, he could go to match-meetings or even to small local shows. Probably the easiest thing is to take him to the park or the nearest town, and sit somewhere where people can stop to talk to him, as they undoubtedly will.

In most cases, socialising will entail a ride in the car, and it is better for both of you if he learns to like the car. Very short trips to places where he is going to really enjoy himself, such as the woods, or the house of a friend who gives him tasty snacks, will help him to think car rides are enjoyable. If the only place he ever goes is to the vet's, it is not surprising if he suffers from travel-sickness.

Most Deerhounds tolerate cars well but, to be on the safe side, (after having a couple that did suffer sickness), I tend to give travel-sickness pills to my puppies the first few times they go in the car, so that they never learn to associate the car with feeling sick.

Collars and leads

By law, a dog is required to wear a collar with identification when he is not on his own premises, so the sooner the puppy gets used to wearing a collar, the better. Mine object only mildly the first couple of times on a lead, and after that accept it as normal. If you treat it in a matter-of-fact way he will accept it more quickly than if you make a big performance out of it.

If you intend to show your Deerhound, he needs to wear his collar as little as possible, because any sort of collar will rub the hair on the neck in time. This completely spoils the outline of the hound. Some people use a wide greyhound-type collar, but this can rub out quite a lot of coat, and I find that a thin, rolled leather collar worn fairly loosely is the least damaging to the coat.

If you intend to attach a lead to the collar, then the collar has to be much tighter, as the Deerhound has a relatively narrow skull compared to his neck, (as an adult anyway), so it is easy for him to slip out of a collar if he pulls backward. Because of this, regardless of whether my Deerhound is wearing a collar or not, I prefer to use a slip lead, which tightens whichever direction he pulls in and therefore is much safer. Slip leads can be made of leather, rope or nylon. The most important consideration is the size of the ring in relation to the width of the lead. The ring diameter should be at least twice that size, or it will tangle in the coat and will not release when the lead is loose.

It is a good idea to make sure your hound always wears his collar, but not lead, in the car. If you have an accident and the hound escapes, it will be easier for someone to catch him and return him to you. However, when leaving him alone in the car, remove his collar as he could get it caught on something and choke. For the same reason, remove his collar when he is playing at home unsupervised.

Most leads have a loop on the end, which makes it easier for the owner to keep hold. However it also means that if the hound gets away from you and runs off wearing his lead, he could catch his foot in the loop and break his leg or neck. Therefore it is better if the lead is long enough to prevent this or if it has a knot on the end instead of a loop.

Flexi-leads can be useful if you wish to allow your hound to run in a public place and are worried that he may not come back to you. They should not be used extended on pavements or along the roadside as the hound could run out into the road or get his lead tangled around legs other than his own.

Exercise

As mentioned before, puppies should be allowed as much rest as they need and should therefore not have enforced lead exercise until they are at least ten months old. Depending on your situation, they can have as much free running and playing as they wish to take, as long as they have access to somewhere to rest when they wish.

A large flat lawn or field is ideal as it is soft to fall on and will not put undue stress on the limbs as hilly or uneven land can do. There is another point of view that uneven land will teach them to be careful of where they put their feet. Perhaps it is best if they have the flat land to start with and the other when they are a bit older.

Some breeders like to have a run with a pebble surface as it is believed that this will help keep the feet tight. In my experience, if they have any option they will not walk on the pebbles, which are uncomfortable. Good feet are bred, not made, and though they sometimes 'go off' between three and six months of age, they should tighten up again if they were good in the first place.

Begin lead exercise with a few hundred yards and build up gradually over weeks rather than days. By the time he is fifteen months old he will be able to take any amount of exercise as long as it is increased in a reasonable way. Even as an adult, it is as unwise to leave a dog unexercised all week then give him a ten mile walk at weekend as it would be with a human, and just as likely to cause muscle strain and stiffness. One of the most important aspects of exercise is that it should be regular, which means a reasonable amount at least once a day.

If you intend to show your Deerhound, then he must be fit and in good condition. Free running exercise will stretch and build up the muscle, especially if it incorporates uphill and downhill work. Running uphill will build up the muscle in the neck, back and hindquarters and downhill will build up the forequarters. If you wish your hound to put some effort into his running, you may have to restrict his free running exercise to twice a week. Being lazy, if he has constant access to free exercise, he is more likely to meander about, sniffing. Two Deerhounds together will get more exercise as they push each other into it. Three is not such a good number as one gets left out and will then try to grab one of the others, causing squabbles, or get in the way and cause an accident. Jumping is also supposed to be good for the hindquarters, but too much could damage the joints in the front legs when the hound lands. You may also be storing up future trouble for yourself as once a hound realises that he can jump, his size means that he can jump more or less anything and you may not be able to keep him in.

Road walking will tighten up the muscles all round, and keep the feet in good shape. Four miles a day, preferably split into two walks, should be ample unless you are trying to get a hound fit for coursing or similar strenuous work. The walking needs to be at a brisk pace to do any good, and the hound should be kept at a steady trot. Hounds made to walk more slowly, when they have to walk alongside a pram, for instance, are sometimes seen to pace, because it is uncomfortable for them to walk for long periods and the speed is not fast enough for them to maintain a trot.

I feel that the capacity to muscle up is largely hereditary. Although it is possible to improve on the muscle tone of any hound, some build up muscle very easily, while others put on very little in relation to the exercise they are given.

If you exercise in an arable area, be aware of crop-spraying, and in all areas roadside spraying, with chemicals, as the hound may lick his legs or feet when he gets home and become ill.

Before allowing your hound to roam free, please make sure that there are no sheep or other animals in sight, and be on your guard in case any appear. If one gets up suddenly under his nose and runs, he will instinctively set off after it before he has time to think whether he should or not, and the farmer may not be as understanding as you would like.

Always be aware that these are sighthounds and, if you have to exercise in a park or other public place, don't let him off the lead unless you know for absolute certainty that he will come back as soon as he is called. You may know that he will not harm the little dog he has just run off to greet, but the sight of such a large hound bearing down on their beloved pet is a frightening sight for most dog-owners and an owner in a panic may worsen the situation considerably. Deerhounds are renowned for their excellent temperaments and we all have a responsibility to ensure that their reputation remains intact.

Temperament

Talking of the Deerhound temperament, it is worth noting the various stages an owner may expect. Deerhounds are very slow-maturing, mentally as well as physically, and should be treated accordingly.

Dogs want to love and trust their owners and will put up with an amazing amount of abuse without complaint. It is up to any owner to try to understand some of the things that go on in their heads, and a better understanding is sure to produce a better relationship. It has been said many times before, but is worth repeating, that the owner must be the pack leader. If the hound can trust you to take charge in every situation, he will be much happier. Therefore it is imperative that he knows his boundaries in everything if he is to grow into a well-adjusted Deerhound. When the dog/human relationship fails, it is virtually always the fault of the owner. The Deerhound wants to please you. All you have to do is to show him how.

All puppies are adorable and so often get away with far too much bad behaviour because they trade on this fact. However this is the best time to start any training because it is infinitely easier to pick up or chase a three month old puppy than an older hound! Having said that, he has not the mental capacity to understand so much and any lessons will have to be simple. Teaching to come when called, and to lie down, should be possible with patience and when he is new to you he is usually delighted with the attention and always willing to come. As he gets older, his natural curiosity gets in the way and he may need to explore what he is doing thoroughly first, before he responds. Lessons learned in the early days will now stand the owner in good stead, because the hound ought to know the difference in your tone of voice as to how urgent the request is.

When you feel he is being deliberately naughty, a severe tone of voice is usually enough to make him pay attention. It is very rarely necessary to smack a Deerhound and does not have much effect. For the most effect, a rolled up newspaper rapped against a wall will usually command his immediate attention. Deerhounds seem to really dislike this noise.

It is probably best to liken puppies to toddlers. They are exploring, unable to distinguish right from wrong and put most things in their mouths. They need to have fragile and dangerous objects removed from their reach and they need patience.

Adolescence is probably the most difficult age, in Deerhounds as in humans. At this time the hound is secure in his home and begins to test out his relationship with other members of his family. He needs to know his position in the hierarchy and it is only natural that he will aim for the highest position unless he is shown the error of his ways. To this end he will try to assert himself with different members of the family, who should respond in a similar way.

At some point in his life, your Deerhound may growl at you. This does not mean that you have a nasty Deerhound - any dog who has something about him may do it at some stage, in the same way that they will do it with their siblings and then with other hounds in the family, (rather like teenagers will answer back). However, it should only happen once or, at the most, twice. Never more than this if you respond immediately. The earlier it happens in his life, the easier it is for the owner, simply because he will be so much smaller and easier to deal with. A confident puppy may 'try it on' at a few weeks old, or may get too aggressive with a litter-mate when playing. At five weeks it is easy to flip the puppy onto his back and hold him by the throat and growl at him, much as his canine mother would do. Puppies very rarely try it twice, and don't bother even when they get older. They learned their lesson very early, and painlessly. Most of the puppies I breed and keep never try it on at all, probably because it is clear to them from the start, that I am pack leader. I know many other breeders who have found the same.

The best way to deal with even the slightest sign of aggression, (lip curling, growling, grabbing the owner's hand - I have never known one actually bite), is to respond immediately. This is the one time when you should not give him the benefit of the doubt. If the puppy is small enough, it is easiest to hold him on his back and shake him, growling at him or saying no, or both. When he has grown too big for that, the best way is to pick him up by the coat, on each side of where the jaw meets the neck, and lift him up - not high enough to hurt him, just enough to lift his front feet slightly off the ground, look him in the eye and tell him no, or growl at him, or shake him. It is best to do all three, so that he is left in no doubt that he has just upset you. Dogs feel less secure with their feet off the ground, so he will listen to you. The harder you are on him the very first time he experiments, the less likely he is to ever try it again. After he has learned this lesson, a simple 'no' will probably be enough in most situations.

(By grabbing the owner's hand, I am not talking of puppies who are teething or of older hounds who sometimes like to hold the owner's hand when walking).

When a puppy changes homes he has a new family to fit into, and unless you have always made it clear where he comes in the pecking order, he needs to find out for himself. As long as you are fore-warned, it will be easier. This does not mean you should go around anticipating trouble. Some will be happy to be under-dogs all their lives. But it is as well to know the situations in which it might occur.

Guarding food or, more especially bones, is one situation in which your puppy might get above his station. This is quite a good situation to deliberately provoke, (especially if there are young children in the house), by giving the puppy a bone, or similar treat, then taking it off him again. He will probably just wag his tail at you, in which case give him back the bone and give him a big cuddle as well. If he gets cross, respond as above.

The other situation that can cause rebellion is the guarding of a chair and is caused by the owner confronting the hound. It may be the hound's own chair, or may be just one that he fancies, but the Deerhound gets himself comfortable and the owner comes in and asks him to get down. He puts on his insolent face. Owner insists, hound refuses. Owner tries to pull hound off chair from the front and hound growls or even turns his head and gets hold of owners arm or hand. Owner has a choice which must be made instantaneously. Owner can back off, (wrong choice as hound has now established right to the chair and will take much more persuading the next time) or owner can spring into action, taking hound by surprise and ensuring a resounding victory.

The easiest way to get a Deerhound out of a chair, when he is being stubborn, is to go round the back of it and tip him out. This avoids any confrontation at all. Then you can either chase him out of the room growling at him, or sit in the chair yourself. The trouble is, he will probably just sit on top of you. A Deerhound apologising is often more trouble than a Deerhound being naughty.

I apologise to those owners who have the natural authority that they and their hounds take for granted. It may be hard for them to believe that there are some owners who are apprehensive of correcting their hounds for fear of retaliation. This creates an unhappy hound and an unhappy owner. The Deerhound may look a big dog, but underneath he's just a big softy who wants to be understood, and wants to respect his owner. Part of his charm is actually this - that he does push his luck quite often. Once he knows his boundaries and he has grown up, allowing him some liberties is what builds his lovely character.

Another situation that occasionally causes a problem is apparent aggression at shows. This is exaggerated because a dog is usually more confident when on a lead. It is very often the same hounds involved because they are misunderstood. If a hound is frequently getting picked on, nine times out of ten it is that hound's fault, even though it doesn't look that way. An owner should be aware of the signals that the hound is giving off all the time. Most Deerhounds greet each other with ears back and tail wagging. You can just tell they are smiling. However if raised ears are accompanied by a stiff, arched neck with prolonged eye contact and a raised tail, this is the time to distract him and growl a warning at him. These are the first signs of aggression and if your hound tries it with a dominant male, he will get put in his place. (It happens much more often with males). Both hounds should be reprimanded, but if the first owner was more observant, it would hardly ever happen. If he does it a second time, then picking him up so that his front feet are slightly off the ground, as explained before, when shouting or growling at him, should get through to him. It really is important that you correct it the first time it happens. The correction must be quick and it must be firm, not the tentative admonishment sometimes seen. Also the hound must listen to you.If he is still looking round you for the other dog, keep correcting him until he listens. Even worse and all too often, one sees the 'picked on' hound getting a cuddle from his owner. This intensifies the problem. This so-called victim started it in most cases.

This is not to be confused with a Deerhound attacking a puppy or another dog that is showing no signs of aggression. This is totally unacceptable and if the owner cannot or will not take steps to prevent it, then the hound in question should not be taken to shows or other events, where it could do untold harm to the confidence of a youngster to which it takes a dislike.

If owners were always one step ahead of their hounds, both would be a lot happier. The above incidents are the only ones I have come across or heard about, and all are caused by a young hound finding his feet and looking for guidance from his owner. Once he can rely on his owner to be the boss, the above problems are unlikely to surface, and in the majority of cases, they don't.

I keep my adult males together and they will happily curl up together asleep when there is an in-season bitch in the next room, without a cross word being spoken and with no attempt being made to get to the bitch. Nor do they squabble if one goes out to mate a visiting bitch and then goes back to his friend. It may be worth mentioning here that if you do keep two males, or two females for that matter, and you know which is the dominant one, if they do have a fight then you must support the dominant one. Support of the under-dog causes confusion between them and gives the under-dog permission to try to assert itself again, causing another fight. A wise owner will prevent a fight by teaching the hounds that even cross words are not acceptable.

All of mine establish their hierarchy without my being aware of it, and get on together in any combination. Because they know their boundaries, I can let them do forbidden things at times, which makes them feel special, but in the knowledge that they will not assume it is a permanent arrangement. Of course they may test their boundaries at any age, but sometimes I think they are just doing it to make sure they can still trust the owner to be the boss. All breeds will do this and Deerhounds are much less trouble than most.

To reiterate, Deerhounds have delightful temperaments, and as long as owners are observant and sensible, there should not be any problems.

Spaying
This is largely a matter of personal choice. If you know for sure that you have no intention of ever having a litter, and your bitch goes everywhere with you, it will make life easier not to have to worry about her coming in season at an inconvenient time. If you intend to show, it is possible to show a bitch who is spayed, with Kennel Club permission, but it may be that you will get interested in your hobby and decide you would like to try to breed something yourself.

If a bitch is spayed, it will prevent her from getting a pyometra. However, in some cases it will make the coat softer and require more grooming to keep it looking well.

Another consideration is that spaying requires a general anaesthetic, which is not without risk.

Castration
It is rare to castrate a male Deerhound, and is usually unnecessary except for medical reasons. Deerhound males are comparatively easy-going and should not need neutering because of temperament problems. Again there is the risk of a general anaesthetic.

Maturity
Deerhounds are not mature until they are about three and a half or four years old, and then will still improve in looks for another year or more. Their character is also developing all the time and the mature hounds are wonderful. By this time they have learned all the rules, and when to break them, how to get round their owners and all the other things that make them such great companions.

Even if fussy eaters as youngsters, by now they should have settled and eat well, which makes life easier for the owner. They will have passed the chewing, though possibly not the stealing, stage.

Even as old-timers, they are adorable, though they are considerably more impatient when they want something and their coats can be thicker and need more care.

The best way to teach them, intentionally or unintentionally, how to do anything is to laugh at them, so by now they will have a whole series of ways of asking for what they want, beginning with sighing, (Deerhounds are great sighers), followed by stamping the feet and tossing the head and finishing with knocking the book or newspaper out of the owner's hand if still being ignored.

Something that they find highly amusing, though the owner may find embarrassing, is choosing unsuitable times to burp, which they do a lot anyway. When the owner is talking on the telephone, they will wander over, place their mouth near to the mouthpiece and give the person on the other end quite a shock. Also when out for a walk, they pick the moment that the owner is passing another walker, and manage a very loud one. The conclusion reached by the passer-by, who has no knowledge of the Deerhound sense of humour, is not a favourable one.

They are very good at disguising themselves as rugs, and don't leap to their feet as someone strides over them which, considering their size, is a very good thing. However they are not averse to sticking out a leg at the last minute to trip someone up. I don't think it is anything personal as they do it to each other as well.

Although they rarely jump, unless taught, they do sometimes take the easy way out, and if you have one that is good at opening latches and catches, then locked padlocks are the only answer. A padlock that is just hooked over is no deterrent at all, nor are rope loops. Some really are Houdinis. Luckily, not many.

If kept with a smaller breed, they seem to prefer the smaller dog's bed and can often be seen with their middle part wedged in and everything else hanging over the edge, looking most uncomfortable.

Most are not too keen on hot weather and can look quite uncomfortable if out in the sun for any length of time. However, light any sort of fire indoors, in any of the eleven coldest months of the year and you will wonder why you can't feel any heat from it, especially if you have more than one Deerhound.

Still, it's a small price to pay.

Ch. Greybrows Moonstorm bred by Mr & Mrs R. Redmond   (Photo by Carol Ann Johnson)

Ch. Beardswood Amalia bred by Mrs H. & Dr S. Helps   (Photo by Robert Gladstone)

Ch. Flaunden Bonnie Mary bred by Mrs J Blandford

Ch.Regalflight Sedge bred by Mrs J. Bond

Chapter Six

FEEDING

There are many different ways of feeding Deerhounds and the more people I ask, the more methods I find. While a few general rules apply, it is largely a matter of finding the food that your Deerhound likes and is convenient for you.

Before the puppy is six months old, it is best to be guided by the puppy's breeder, but after that time the puppy should be settled with you and any changes can be made, but should always be made gradually.

Good condition relies on the owner to be observant and note if the hound is losing weight or getting too fat. Again, different owners have their own preference as to how much weight the hound should carry. Some very fit hounds are actually quite thin, but it is also possible for a hound to have more weight and still be fit. For showing it is probably most acceptable to most judges if the ribs are well-covered but still easily felt.

The condition is also dependent on the temperament and age of the hound. Some hounds are very laid-back, eat well and seem to maintain condition whatever happens, while others do not have such a good appetite, still manage to be twice as energetic and run off the benefits of what little food they do eat. Just like people. In general, Deerhounds are not greedy feeders. Dogs will usually require more food than bitches.

Water
Water is the most essential requirement of any dog, and should always be clean, and therefore emptied and replaced a few times a day. More will be necessary if a complete dry food is fed.

Quality
Always buy the best quality food you can afford. This is especially true while the puppy is still growing, which is until around eighteen months old. Cheap food is cheap for a reason. Meat may contain parts of the animal that upset your hound's stomach. Cereal products may be bulked up with ingredients that are unsuited to dogs. These foods contain variable ingredients, relying on whatever is cheap at the time of manufacture and you will not be able to identify which one is causing problems. The main companies standardise the ingredients of their products and have a reputation to consider. They can offer help and will be genuinely concerned if you are having problems.

Exercise

Deerhounds, like people, should not have strenuous exercise within an hour of feeding, either before or after. After a meal, a greater supply of blood than normal is directed to the stomach to aid digestion, and when exercising the blood is needed elsewhere. At the very least it will cause discomfort. Puppies, of course, don't know the rules and a meal often seems to stimulate them into activity, though it is best to try to persuade them to rest.

Temperature

If living outside, Deerhounds will require more food when the weather is cold, as some extra food will be needed to maintain body temperature.

Conventional Diets

People still think of a conventional diet as meat and biscuit, with the addition of milk and eggs at times, and many people still feed this way, probably because they think of dogs as carnivores. Dogs are actually omnivores and meat alone is not enough and is not balanced. If feeding meat, tripe or similar, it must be mixed with at least half the amount of biscuit, terrier meal or brown bread. This type of diet will probably still be deficient in vitamins and minerals and so a multivitamin supplement should be given daily, something like Canovel or Pet-tabs, with additional cod-liver oil in winter. Eggs should be cooked if fed in quantity, as raw egg white binds certain vitamins, causing vitamin deficiency, though one raw egg a day should not cause a problem.

Fresh frozen meat and tripe is now available from a number of suppliers nationwide, as well as from some butchers, and can be bought in convenient packs.

One to one-and-a-half pounds (450 to 700grams) of meat per day should be enough for an adult Deerhound, though the amount of biscuit or other mixer fed varies considerably from breeder to breeder asked - anything from half a pound (250g) of biscuit or cheap complete food to two pounds (900g) of top quality biscuit, and most fed it in one meal, though the time of day varied.

Most breeders who feed meat cook it, which helps kill any bacteria or parasites. Breeders who feed tripe rather than meat, tend to feed it raw, probably because of the smell when cooking.

Tinned meat

This is a more convenient way to obtain meat and should be fed in accordance with the suggestions of the manufacturer unless your hound is losing or putting on weight, in which case it should be adjusted accordingly. Again it should be fed with at least half the quantity of good biscuit or mixer made specifically for this purpose.

Moist foods
These are sold in packets and on the advertisements always look delicious, but I have no knowledge, first or second-hand, of these products. They might be useful to take away on holiday, or in similar situations, as they seem more convenient than tins, but if you wish to do this, try out the product first at home to make sure it suits your hound.

Complete dry foods (extruded biscuit-type, not flake)
These have recently become a very popular way of feeding dogs, easily available in many types of recipe, at various prices and for every stage of a dog's life. They are convenient, time-saving foods and easy to handle.

These foods vary greatly in composition and quality. For the purpose of feeding Deerhounds, it is a good idea to read the instructions before you buy and choose one of the top quality ones that require feeding a smaller amount of food. This will not overload the stomach, will give the same amount of nutrition as twice the amount of a cheap food and will produce half the amount of clearing up at the other end! From this point of view, they are a good idea for fussy hounds who refuse to eat much, as some of the top brands have a daily ration of only fourteen ounces (400 grams) which, if split into two feeds, does not require much perseverance on the part of the hound. Because the hound needs a smaller amount, they can actually work out less expensive than some of the cheap foods, and are usually more palatable.

The food can be fed soaked or dry. If dry, a drop of water can be added just before serving to moisten slightly.

The manufacturers of these products spend a great deal of money in research and in balancing their foods. It is therefore unnecessary and undesirable to add meat or anything else which then makes them unbalanced. If you wish to feed this type of food and your hound needs more encouragement to eat, then only the smallest amount of anything should be added, and usually just moistening the meal is enough.

Flaked foods
All breeders I asked did not feed flaked food. Because of the lower protein content it is usually necessary to feed it in large quantities, which would tend to overload the stomach.

Supplements
Any vitamin supplement should be given in moderation, and is only necessary with conventional diets, as mentioned. Puppies fed on conventional diets may also need extra calcium and cod-liver oil. There is a far greater risk in feeding too many vitamins and too much calcium, which misguided owners sometimes do with the idea that more is better. When feeding a complete balanced diet, supplementation of any sort is not to be recommended and may be harmful.

Variety

Giving your hound a variety of food is not necessary, as long as the food is balanced. The bacteria in the dog's digestive tract are designed to cope with the same food day in day out, so that changing the diet is not actually helpful.

The fussy eater

There are quite a lot of fussy Deerhounds about, and most belong to owners who allow them to be fussy. This does not matter to anyone who likes going to a lot of trouble thinking up new things to feed each day, but most owners like feeding-time to be straight forward.

The trouble usually begins when the Deerhound is a puppy. The new owner is very aware that the hound has a lot of growing to do, so when the hound will not eat, the owner becomes worried. The hound senses this and plays the owner up, either intentionally or not. As mentioned in the puppy chapter, Deerhounds are sensitive to their owner's feelings and a worrying owner will produce a worrying Deerhound. It isn't always apparent to the Deerhound whether the owner wants him to eat or not, because if he pauses, the food is taken away and changed. Does this mean there was something wrong with the other food? he thinks. Alternatively he learns to wait to see if the next offering is more to his liking. A hovering owner makes him wonder if he is doing something wrong.

Difficult as it is, the only way is to ignore him. If, after ten minutes, he hasn't finished, throw the food away and offer similar, but in a smaller quantity next meal. The idea should be to give him less and less until you find the amount he will eat happily and stick to that for a while, until he learns to eat. If he eats, do not give any more at that meal. That is no sort of reward for him. Telling him he's a clever boy is a better idea.

There are various products on the market said to improve appetite. Sometimes the B vitamins are suggested, and brewer's yeast may help.

One of the good things about a complete diet is that it does not matter if the hound is picking over his food. Even if he eats a small amount, it will still be balanced. If he is fed a conventional diet, he will probably pick out the bits he likes, which is not good for him in the long term.

It is best to feed the Deerhound in a matter-of-fact way, making no comment when he eats or when he leaves his food. Simply throw it away and carry on with whatever you were doing.

The above tips will work in almost every case. As soon as the owner genuinely stops worrying, (as opposed to just saying he isn't bothered), the hound will eat. It may take a few months before the owner genuinely does get fed up, but he will eventually.

In very rare cases, the personality of the hound is just too stubborn. I have had two bitches who have virtually lived on fresh air. The first one was the more normal kind - I fussed over her and offered her a variety of tasty morsels, (I hadn't learned any better in those days), until I eventually gave up and ignored her and she started eating normally. Any subsequent ones were cured by being ignored, until I met my match in Cassie, who ate very little for three years. Eventually I gave in to her insistence that she isn't really a dog, and she agreed to eat breakfast out of my cereal bowl, (after I've finished), and to eat some dinner if there is an extra something on top, she doesn't mind what. We got on much better after that, I suppose we understood each other better, and she put weight on. When she was pregnant, however, she had to have all her meals on one of our plates - no type of dog bowl was good enough. She is back to eating out of dog bowls again now, and luckily all of her children eat well. (And I will definitely not do it again!).

Most bitches can go off their food about two to three weeks after a season, but usually resume eating their usual amount again at around six weeks. This is normal and is due to hormonal changes in the body at this time. There is no need to worry unless the hound is already thin, in which case it will be necessary to tempt her with something tastier.

The poor doer

Sometimes a hound will eat quite well and yet not put any weight on. Once you have checked for worms and that there is nothing physically wrong with him, it may be an idea to change his diet. If you feed a complete food, and your hound likes it, take advice from the manufacturer on which food from their range to feed. An alternative is to go for a higher protein food, as long as it doesn't give him so much energy that he runs off all the extra goodness. Increase the fat content of his food by adding suet, or other sorts of fat from the butcher's, or a small amount of cooking oil to his food, as long as it does not upset his stomach. If you really want to treat him, breast of lamb is excellent at putting on weight and always much appreciated.

If you feed only one meal, try splitting his ration into two meals as I believe this is more likely to maintain weight than one meal.

The above applies to adult hounds. Immature hounds often look rather rangy because they are still growing upward and lengthways, and will not start to fill out until their growth slows down.

The overweight hound
This is not much of a problem in Deerhounds. Sometimes older bitches or spayed bitches can have a tendency to put on too much weight if not kept on strict rations, and the amount needed to maintain their ample proportions is such a tiny amount that they can look at you in disbelief. Mixing vegetables into their food helps to bulk it up while adding very few calories, and will also help to slow down their eating, which helps convince them that they are not being starved.

Ch. Wickwar Misty Willow bred by Mrs Sue Reynolds

Greystiel Garva bred by Miss A Smart

Chapter Seven

HOUSING

This book is about living with Deerhounds and therefore is mainly concerned with Deerhounds living in the house. While there are many people who have Deerhounds who live out, I feel this is not really living with them. There is no doubt that the Deerhounds can be happy and healthy kept in this way, but the owners are missing out on such a lot. Deerhounds develop more character by their constant correlation with their owners, and though the kennel hounds may have a great deal of charm, their owners will not always see it. However, the book would not be complete without looking at ways of keeping hounds outdoors, and in other ways.

By kennels, most owners mean loose-boxes or sheds, usually with their own run attached. Runs are not a substitute for exercising the hounds, and confinement of hounds to kennels and runs would create boredom.

Living Quarters

The best sort of kennels I have seen consisted of a range of loose-boxes around a gravel stable-yard. The doors were halved, and also had an inner door of mesh so that the outer door could be left open and the dogs could see out into the yard and watch what was going on without the need to stand on their hind legs to see over the half-door. The rear of the boxes opened onto a grass paddock, so that it was very easy to give the dogs either gravel exercise or galloping on grass, and the open aspect prevented the dogs from ever getting bored. This was as close as I have seen to the ideal, and very few of us could hope to achieve this.

The choice of materials for the building will probably be dependent on money available. Stone or brick buildings will be more attractive, warmer in winter, cooler in summer and not easily damaged by the occupants. They are very expensive, however, and require skill in construction. For these reasons, most owners have to make do with timber kennels.

If you have a choice of where to site your kennel, aspect will probably depend on how your garden is situated, and how much shelter there is. If the door faces north or east it will get the cold winds and snow blowing in. If it faces south or west it will probably get the wet and windy weather, so will probably need other protection as well. A doorway facing south, with provision to close the top of the door in bad weather, plus a shaded area for the hound to keep out of the sun will be fine.

I think it unkind to keep one hound permanently on its own outside, so I will assume there will be two living together. The shed needs to be at least six feet by eight feet, (2 x 2.7m), so that there will be room for a bed and a small area to move around if the hounds are shut in for any reason.

The bed should be large enough for both hounds to lie down comfortably when stretched out. If it is possible to have a larger shed, then it would be best to have a large bed for them to lie together plus a smaller bed away from the other in case there were any arguments and one hound would not let the other on the shared bed. It is debatable whether the bed should be raised or not. For puppies, it would be best at floor level, with a slight lip round it to keep in the bedding, as puppies spend a lot of time racing each other up and down the run and will bounce on and off the bed at the same time. For adults it is better raised a little off the floor to keep the occupants out of any draughts.

A window will let in more light and make it more pleasant for the hounds and easier for the owner to work in, but should ideally be on the north side so that the sun does not make the kennel unbearably hot. It should also be covered on the inside with fine wire mesh, so that if the hounds jump up against it with any force, there will be no likelihood of them actually breaking the glass.

The roof of the kennel needs to be high enough so that the owner can stand upright to facilitate cleaning and make life easier.

It goes without saying that the kennel needs to be water-tight, and it will make it more pleasant in both summer and winter if it is insulated all round, especially the roof.

The floor is the most difficult, and it is largely a matter of preference and of trial and error to find a type of floor that suits you. Concrete, painted with a waterproof finish, is relatively easy to clean but is cold. Wood is warmer but harder to clean, even if it is varnished or covered with sawdust. A covering of lino or similar is suitable if the hounds are older and not likely to chew it, and even carpet, renewed regularly, would be nice if the hounds are likely to keep it clean.

All door catches should be easy to operate and placed, as far as it is possible, out of reach of the occupants. It is also a good idea to cover any wooden edges with metal capping if you are able to obtain it, as wood is a great delicacy to puppies, and often older hounds too. (Having said that, quite a few like the taste of metal!).

Bedding

In winter, most people use straw or shredded paper to a depth of about a foot (30cm). The hound can dig his way into this and keep warm. Straw is cheaper and usually easier to obtain, and paper is better for hounds or owners who suffer from allergies. Both will gradually break down and should be renewed regularly.

In summer, any of the types of bedding used in the house would be suitable.

Lighting and Heating

It will be a great help in winter if the kennel is wired for electric lighting and heating. It is not very convenient to try to feed or clean out the hounds while holding a torch in one hand. All wiring must be in a suitable conduit and well out of the way of curious noses. I am rather wary of having any sort of heat lamp suspended over a bed unless it is absolutely secure as one occasionally hears of lamps being knocked onto bedding causing fires, and fatalities. There are special kennel heaters which are wall-mounted and should be safer, though I have no first-hand knowledge of these. If the kennel is attached to the house, it may be possible to plumb in a radiator, which would be ideal.

Healthy adults, carrying enough weight, living outside permanently and with ample bedding should not need artificial heat. Some owners, however, have their hounds in the house during the day and outside at night, in which case the contrast in temperatures would mean the hound would probably feel the cold at night and would need extra heat.

Runs

The run may as well be as large as you have room for, within reason, and I have seen runs of all sizes. If the run is only for occasional use, the size is not so important. If the hounds are to spend most of their life out there, it should be much larger, possibly twelve by five yards (or metres). There should also be a large grass paddock for running exercise and the hound should be taken out for a walk at least once a day.

Grass runs are fine for adults if the land is free-draining and the hounds do not dig. Usually grass runs become mud-yards in winter and full of holes, which could be dangerous. A permanent surface is more satisfactory and easier to clean. Gravel is a cheap solution but, unless it has a hard surface underneath, it will gradually sink into the earth and will need to be renewed regularly. Weeds will grow up through it and look unsightly unless a membrane is put underneath the gravel. However, Deerhounds still tend to dig in gravel and will mix it with the earth underneath or damage the membrane. With either grass or gravel runs, it is best to have a flag or concrete path all the way round the edge to stop them trying to dig their way out, and this will also take most of the wear.

The parts of the run which will get the most use are the points where the hounds can observe their owners approach, or watch the family coming and going.

Runs with a paving or concrete surface are the most durable and easiest to clean, and can be disinfected to help prevent smells and the spread of disease.

Raised timber platforms in the runs are appreciated by hounds for both sunbathing and for playing on. Various indestructible toys will be appreciated and will help prevent boredom.

Fencing

Around the run the fencing should be substantial as the hounds have unlimited time to find a way out. The metal panels, with or without doors, designed specifically for the purpose and advertised regularly in the dog papers, are by far the best. They are rigid, strong, indestructible and easy to erect and bolt together.

The next best fencing is probably chain link, as long as the support posts are set firmly in the ground and the wires are strained. Gates or doors substantial enough to cope with the wear and tear are difficult to build in this sort of construction. Deer fencing, or two rows of sheep fencing one on top of the other, would be other alternatives, though not very attractive, but other types of wire mesh are not really strong enough for this sort of use.

If the run is bounded by a solid wall, the gate should be mesh all the way to the ground so that the hounds can see out at some point. For the same reason, if the mesh panels are solid at the bottom, it should only be to a height of two feet, (60 cm), so that the hounds can see out, or they will spend a lot of time standing on their hind legs trying to see what is going on.

Other accommodation

Deerhounds are very adaptable and will fit into any situation as long as they are loved and cared for. The more facilities an owner has, in the way of a large house, large garden, paddock for exercise, a beach or rural surroundings in which the hound may be exercised freely, the better, (in theory), will be the life of their Deerhound. It has to be said, too, that there are some breeders who will not sell to buyers with anything less than this.

However, just because you have none of these things does not necessarily mean that you should forget the idea of owning your own Deerhound. It does mean that you will have to expend a lot more effort and take a lot more care in his day-to-day life and the whole exercise will be much more time-consuming than if you had the ideal facilities. In other words, you will have to be a special sort of person to spend most of your spare time in making his life a happy one. But most people who lack the right facilities realise this, and it is often said that big breeds who live in flats and have a lot of care taken over them are much fitter than some of those whose owners have a big garden and think the dog can look after itself.

Chapter Eight

GENERAL CARE

Grooming

The Deerhound coat is very easy to take care of and a thorough weekly grooming should be enough to keep it looking and feeling good. Most owners say they prefer the look of the hound when he has not been groomed for a while, but that is not an excuse for allowing the coat to get matted. It is a matter of preference which position the hound should be in. If your Deerhound likes to be brushed, then it will be kinder to your back if he will stand (still). Otherwise it may be easier with the hound lying on his side.

It is best to start puppies with a soft bristle brush, be gentle and make the whole thing fun. Some Deerhounds have quite sensitive skin, especially over the ribs and stomach, and allowing these to get matted and then subjecting the hound to rough brushing will result in a hound who disappears as soon as he sees you open the drawer in which the grooming equipment is kept.

When the adult coat comes through, either a similar brush with stiffer bristles, or a padded brush with metal teeth, (preferably with rounded or 'bobble' ended teeth), will be kindest to the coat, and to him. A 'slicker' brush, with fine bent metal teeth, will get through a thick coat more quickly but will take out more of the undercoat, and hurts the skin unless used with care.

Combs are useful for going over the coat after brushing, and will find all the bits that have been missed. They will tease out knots, which are best held away from the skin by the other hand while combing, so that they do not keep tugging at the skin.

Those small, fine knots in the more sensitive areas, on the stomach and inside the hind legs, are best cut off with nail-scissors, while making sure the hound keeps very still.

From time to time, the coat on some Deerhounds may appear longer and take on a reddish tinge. This coat is dead coat and is best removed, either by combing over with a stripping comb, or simply by removing the dead coat with your fingers. It is best done a little at a time.

Grooming for showing will be covered in the next chapter. If you do not wish to show then the above is sufficient, although removing the long, fine hairs on the ears will improve the appearance and will not be objected to if done a few at a time when the hound is resting.

Bathing

Bathing is not really necessary for a hound that lives in the house and most Deerhounds have little smell, if they are brushed regularly and have somewhere clean to sleep. Occasionally, however, the hound may roll in something unsavoury and it may be necessary to bath him.

Indoors or out, the water used should be tepid. Cold water will not encourage the hound to co-operate, and hot water may give him a chill. If the weather is warm, it is easiest to bath him in the garden, using the hosepipe or jugs of water. If not, a bath with a shower attachment is ideal, as long as you can persuade the hound to get into the bath, and if afterwards you can get him out through the house before he floods it out. A downstairs bathroom with a separate shower would be ideal if you are in the process of designing your house at the moment. Once actually in the bath they tend to tolerate it without any fuss. Always use a dog shampoo or a mild baby shampoo, not your own shampoo which may be too harsh. Whichever is used, it should be rinsed thoroughly, unless using an insecticidal shampoo, in which case follow the manufacturer's instructions.

Towel him as dry as possible and then release somewhere safe and stand back!

Nails

For some Deerhounds, road work is enough to keep their nails short, but this is not always the case and, like people, some Deerhounds' nails grow faster than others and need regular trimming.

There are various clippers on the market and it is a matter of personal preference which to use. Guillotine types need to be the jumbo size as adult nails can be quite thick and hard. Strong nail-clippers are another option, also a strong rasp or an electric grinding tool. It depends on which you find easiest to use and which the hound least objects to.

Like grooming, nail-clipping can be done with the hound standing, holding up one paw at a time, or with the hound lying down, which most people prefer. If possible, shave off a little at a time until the hound lets you know that you are getting close to the quick, (the pink triangular part inside the nail, easily visible on white nails but not on dark nails). It is more difficult with a hound who objects, as it is necessary to get the job done as quickly as possible and you may have to cut it off in one go. Unfortunately this usually makes the hound object more as it seems to be the noise of the clippers, as much as anything, that they don't like. It is a frustrating job as, just as you have positioned the clippers on the nail, the foot is snatched away. Like other unpleasant tasks, it is easier if they are taught to accept it as puppies.

If the hound has also to be bathed, the nails are easier to cut afterwards, when softer. Also, don't forget to cut the dew claws along with the others.

Ears

Most Deerhounds have ears that stay pink and clean all their lives, and are healthy because of the shape and good air circulation. Some produce more wax, which attracts dirt and debris and means that they need a wipe over occasionally. It is best to check each time the hound is groomed, and remove any excess gently with a tissue or cotton bud. Do not go into the ear beyond the part you can easily see. If the hound is scratching his ear a lot or shaking his head or looking uncomfortable, he needs to go to the vet for an examination. Sometimes the ear flap can get dirty on the inside and needs gentle washing, (only the flap).

Teeth

Puppies cut their milk teeth at around three weeks old and by the time they are ready to lose them at four months, the teeth look tiny. This is because the hounds have done an awful lot of growing in the intervening three months, and not because they are short of calcium or they have some serious disease, as one vet informed a lady to whom I sold a puppy when she went in for the vaccinations, (yes, honestly). Between four and six months, the adult teeth will replace the milk teeth and the Deerhound will finish up with forty-two teeth - six incisors top and bottom, two canine teeth top and bottom, eight premolars top and bottom, and the rest molars, four top and six bottom. Deerhounds rarely have missing teeth but, if so, it will probably be one of the premolars.

If fed mainly soft food, there may be a build up of tartar on the surface of the teeth which needs to be removed or it will eventually lead to gum disease, which will cause bad breath and eventual loss of teeth. The easiest way, once it has formed, is to scrape it off with a coin. Alternatively it can apparently be prevented by brushing the teeth regularly with a toothbrush and special canine toothpaste. Chewing on bones, hard biscuits, rasks or chews can also help keep the teeth clean.

Precautions around the house

Having a puppy or growing dog around is like having a toddler and any dangerous items, especially medicines and chemicals, must be locked away.

Wiring is a favourite with some hounds and the results could be fire or death. If the wiring cannot be tacked out of the way, then some sort of barrier is needed. If a circuit breaker is fitted, then at least the chewing should not prove fatal.

Some detergents and carpet cleaners cause allergies so, if your hound suddenly gets itchy skin, check if you have changed any of your cleaners, or your washing powder.

Gardening with Deerhounds

Deerhounds love to help in the garden, and are great at digging, dead-heading, (and live-heading, unfortunately), slug control and watering. If only they could be trained to do these things in the right place, life would be easy.

As in the house, all chemicals must be kept safely out of their way, and should be the sort that are safe to use when there are children in the garden.

I believe some slugs carry a disease that can be fatal to dogs, so Deerhounds should be discouraged from eating them. Obviously all slug bait should be put where a nosy hound cannot uncover it by accident.

A lot of quite common garden plants are poisonous, so care should be taken when choosing new shrubs, flowers and bulbs.

It is very difficult to stop Deerhounds from digging, especially in newly dug earth, where something has just been planted. It may be necessary to fence off areas temporarily, or place flat stones around the roots of new shrubs, until they get established.

It is better not to use cocoa-shell mulch in the garden as, like chocolate, it contains theobromine, which is toxic to dogs even in quite small amounts.

If you are lucky enough to own a swimming-pool, it needs to be fenced unless there are steps that could be used by a hound to get out. Many a dog has been found drowned in a pool because there was no way to escape.

Ch. Stranwith Reason bred by Kay Barret
Joint male record holder with 23 CC's

Ch. Rotherwood Brandon bred by Miss A.N. Hartley   (Photo by Fall)
Joint male record holder with 23 CC's

Ch. Rosslyn Carric bred by Bryan Doak (Photo by David Dalton)
Breed record holder with 40 CC's

Ch. Killoeter Onich bred by Nell & Seumas Caine
Joint male record holder with 23 CC's

Chapter Nine

SHOWS

Showing can be an enjoyable and rewarding hobby, though not financially, I hasten to add. In fact it is rather expensive and can be very frustrating. Before embarking whole-heartedly on a showing 'career' it is worth visiting some shows, at various levels, to see what it entails. We have all watched the group judging at Crufts on television, and been dazzled by the lights and the atmosphere, but most shows are not like that. Many, even at championship level, are held in a muddy field in a howling gale. It sounds exciting to listen to exhibitors discussing travelling to Edinburgh or Bath or other delightful places, and imagining a glamorous life-style. What the exhibitors actually mean is that they are going to a field near Edinburgh this week, and a field near Bath next week. The fields could actually be anywhere, it just takes more petrol to get to some than others.

If this still appeals to you, the next, and most important consideration, is how you will feel when you don't win. By the law of averages, you are going to lose more than you win, at least to start with and probably for ever. Will this affect your attitude to your hound? It is said that there is an eighty per cent turn over of exhibitors every five years, which means that a lot of people give up before they ever get round to winning. I believe, however, that anyone can win with almost any Deerhound if they are prepared to learn, and apply that knowledge with intelligence and perseverance.

Your own Deerhounds are more beautiful than anyone else's, of course they are Surprisingly some judges will not agree, and instead they will put inferior specimens higher up the line. All judges do this at some time or another, (see following section). They can't help it and it is something you have to learn to live with. As long as you still take the best hounds home with you at the end of the day, that is all that matters.

On the plus side, it is the best way to meet other people who share your love of Deerhounds, who will be happy to talk about the subject indefinitely. It is a wonderful chance to learn and, if you are prepared to listen, many more experienced exhibitors will be happy to help you.

There cannot be many hobbies where one can meet people from literally all walks of life, and meet them as equals. In dogs, it does not matter if you are rich and famous in your outside profession, all that matters is what you know about dogs. The world of dogs is a great leveller.

How to start

If you want your Deerhound to be noticed in the ring, then he must stand out and he must look like a typical Deerhound. The only way to know how your Deerhound should look is to know the breed standard thoroughly. There are no short cuts to this. Although experience at looking at many hounds will teach a lot, it is perfectly possible to see a fairly large class of Deerhounds, all of which exhibit the same fault. Without knowledge of the standard, it would be possible to assume that a particular fault is correct.

Compare your own hound against the standard and see what conclusions you arrive at before asking anyone else. Having done that, the breeder of your Deerhound is the best person to talk to. Ask them to point out the virtues and faults of your hound and discuss the best ways to deal with them. It is only good manners to ask the breeder's advice rather than anyone else's, and naturally they have a vested interest in your showing the hound to its best advantage. Occasionally one hears of breeders who will not help, or maybe do not have the knowledge to advise, in which case you could not be blamed for asking someone else whose advice you value.

Attend some shows and pay attention to each class, with the standard in mind. Try to see why the winning hounds are placed over the others and then go home and apply what you have learned.

Age to show

If you have bought your Deerhound specifically to show, then you will be eager to get him into the ring. Do try to be patient - we have all been through that stage and wisdom comes only with hindsight. Taking the puppy to one or two shows within a reasonable distance will not do him too much harm, as long as he is able to sleep as much as possible during the day and is not dragged round all the trade stands, or trotted up and down a lot to practise. By this I mean one or two shows during the six months he is in puppy classes. I have seen many puppies spoiled by too many shows. The first twelve months are very important in his development, and undue stress at this time will reduce his chances of growing to his full potential. Puppies are best at home, playing and sleeping.

After twelve months, when his growth has slowed down, he is having more exercise at home and is mentally better able to cope, it is possible to increase the number of shows. Junior bitches often go through an attractive phase, which is difficult to catch when show entries close so far in advance, but dogs usually look gangly and uncouth. There is no point in taking him to a show if he is looking dreadful, as people will remember him like that. Learn to look at him objectively and imagine him standing in a line with other Deerhounds. In the same way, try to watch him moving, both toward and away from you. If his movement is wayward at the moment, it is better to wait until it has settled down.

The foregoing points also apply to older hounds. Although everyone knows that Deerhounds change throughout their life, and can vary from one show to another in a very short space of time, not everyone takes an objective view at each show. Therefore always try to show your Deerhound at his best, and try to be honest with yourself about how much your Deerhound enjoys showing. If he really hates it, why punish him? Shows are actually very enjoyable if visited without your hounds and all the accompanying paraphernalia.

Many Deerhounds find showing a bore!

How to enter
Shows are advertised in the weekly dog papers. It may be best to start with a local open show, to give the hound some practice and help overcome your nerves. If possible, especially with a puppy, choose an outdoor show, as the indoor ones can be noisy and crowded and not always an enjoyable experience for a first outing.

Whatever type of show it is, send for the schedule in plenty of time, be advised by your breeder which class to enter, and send off the entry, after having double-checked everything on the form. The definitions of all the classes will be in the schedule, and these need to be read carefully each time you enter a show until you know them without looking. Another thing that needs to be read carefully before signing is the declaration that you will abide by the rules and regulations of the show and of the Kennel Club, (which can be obtained in full from the Kennel Club, and some of which are printed in the schedule), and that you will not take to the show any dog which has been ill or in contact with any other dogs who have been ill, during a specified length of time. It is disappointing how many exhibitors ignore this rule, (whether they deliberately flout it, or simply don't read it before signing, I don't know), and talk at shows of the fact that their dog has been poorly the week before.

Preparation
Your Deerhound needs to be willing to move alongside you in the ring. Most judges require the exhibitors to move round the ring together anti-clockwise, (therefore your Deerhound should be on your left), to start with and then, as they assess each hound individually, they ask for a triangle and then a straight line up and down the ring. It is a good idea to practise this at home, or when out for a walk, until the hound will move at your pace on a loose lead, with his head up. He also needs to stand still for a short period of time, which will require training or bribery, (though knowing that you have a favourite morsel in your pocket may distract him too much). If you have a large mirror that you could put on the floor at home, practise standing him in front of it. What you see in the mirror is, more or less, what the judge will see. An alternative is to incorporate a suitable shop-window into your daily walk, although it may take more nerve to do that in a busy high street than in a show-ring!

As you will now have learned the standard, you will have a reasonable idea of which points to enhance on your Deerhound, and you need to work on these well before the show. In addition to his normal grooming, you need to reveal the short, velvety coat on the ears, so any long, fine hairs should be removed. Most hounds will let you do this with finger and thumb, which is the most satisfactory, but for those who fidget it will be quicker to use a stripping comb held against your thumb. Work quickly and as gently as possible and don't attempt too much at once. The hairs stick out and are easier to remove if the flap of the ear is folded around a finger of the opposite hand.

The feet should be tight and well-knuckled so, if they have long hair sticking out on top or round the edge it needs to be removed. Again, do it gradually so that you don't leave bald patches. If, on the other hand, your hound has flat feet, you would be better to trim the hair around the edges of the feet, but leave some sticking up on top. The nails must be short.

The hair should not be removed from the face as there should be a moustache and beard. However, if there is a lot of thick hair around the throat it can give the hound a stuffy appearance and could be thinned out slightly. Going to extremes can make the hound look odd and remember that the coat will take a while to grow back if you make any bad mistakes, so proceed with caution. On some of the very light-coated hounds, the coat comes in black to start with, so your mistakes can look even more obvious later on! Do not take out too much hair down the neck as this makes it look as if you have not read the standard at all. The Deerhound should have a mane. Your puppy may not have much at the moment but an adult male with a good mane is an impressive sight.

Some exhibitors remove the coat all along the underline of the hound, but Deerhounds look better with a deep brisket and so, if you feel the need to remove any, it is best reserved for the tuck-up. This should just be tidied and the line should still be a smooth curve. If it looks as if you have trimmed the underneath, you have gone too far. Male hounds need to be trimmed around the sheath as they can get quite straggly and smelly in this area. They just need a little tuft to help their aim, which isn't all that good at the best of times.

Apart from that, the Deerhound coat can be left as it is. If your hound has a bad fault that could be disguised by the removal of some hair, then experimenting may enhance his appearance, though this is not something that you need to try at first. The object is to create a good first impression. During the detailed examination, a judge should be able to detect the virtues and faults, regardless of any disguises.

The Deerhound should have a natural, ragged appearance and deviating from this fact to any extent is definitely not desirable.

The night before the show, give him a thorough grooming so that he will not need so much at the show. Prepare your show bag, not forgetting show passes, water and water-bowl grooming equipment, food or snacks. Then try to get a good night's sleep!

At the show

Arrive in plenty of time, and settle your Deerhound on his bench, or in some suitable corner if the show is not benched. Groom him so that he is more or less ready to take in the ring and collect your catalogue and ring-number, where necessary. (Some ring-numbers are given out in the ring). Catalogues are rather expensive nowadays, but are invaluable sources of information for newcomers, who will be interested in learning the breeding of the other Deerhounds present, to build up a picture of which ones are related, either to each other or to the owner's hound.

Watch the judge to see what is required of each exhibitor. When the class before your own is about to go into the ring, give your hound a final brush over and take him for some exercise to get him loosened up and alert. When you go into the ring, stand towards the end of the line-up so that you have time to watch the other exhibitors moving and know what to do. If your hound is still a puppy, it may be difficult to keep him still as the judge is going over him, as most puppies are over-friendly and just want to lick the judge. I am sure most do not mind as long as the licking isn't too exuberant! Do not talk to the judge, unless you have been asked a question, (or maybe to apologise if your puppy knocks him over). When the judge is making his final decision, try to stand your hound looking his best, but have one eye on the judge at the same time. Sometimes a Deerhound will only stand still for a few seconds, in which case let him relax if the judge isn't actually looking at him.

All this may seem a lot to remember at first. The main thing that bothers new exhibitors is the thought that everyone will be watching them. Sorry, but the only reasons you will be even noticed at all are if you win, (in which case you will not mind), or if you wear something really unsuitable. Otherwise spectators will be far more interested in your

Deerhound.

Talking of clothes, it is best to wear something comfortable, unobtrusive and in a colour that will complement your hound. Trousers are usually more suitable, in case of high winds or prying noses. Choose shoes in which you can run easily. The hound should also wear an unobtrusive lead. Leather slip leads in brown or black look best, but are very expensive. Fine rope leads in black or natural are the next best thing. Fluorescent pink nylon leads are less than suitable, but may be useful for walking on roads in the dark.

Handling

This section is a case of 'do as I say, not as I do'. Although I have had a couple of Deerhounds that did not much like showing, in general mine enjoy themselves. They, (especially the boys), gaze up happily, tails wagging, legs everywhere and, as I like them to enjoy themselves I am reluctant to be hard enough on them to make them behave. Instead I laugh at them, which makes them even worse. On the other hand, there are some exhibitors who are very strict with their hounds and insist on good behaviour. Their hounds, depending on individual temperament, stand rigidly and behave or go to pieces and will not show at all. Neither of these extremes is ideal.

Most Deerhounds do not fit into either category, but are typical of the criticism levelled at them by exhibitors in other breeds, who say they are boring. They lie around the ring fast asleep, rouse themselves to go round the ring, head down and slouching, stand with a dull expression in their eyes, and dive out of the ring again as soon as possible to resume their nap!

There must be a happy medium, and I would be very pleased to hear from anyone who has the answer! I can only tell you the best way to go about it. When at shows, watch exhibitors who have been in the breed for a while, decide on one or two who you think show well and sympathetically, and try to follow the way in which they do it. By this I mean in sympathy with the individual hound and with the breed as a whole.

As a natural breed, Deerhounds should be shown in a natural manner, standing four-square or with the hind leg nearer the judge slightly further back than the hind leg nearer the handler. When moving, they should move willingly alongside their handler on a loose lead. Stringing them up with a lead held tightly under the chin, makes them move mincingly as a toy breed or a terrier, instead of really striding out. It also spoils the correct outline, as the head is in an unnatural position. Watch your hound standing and moving at home, naturally, and note in which position he looks his best. Some Deerhounds look better moving at a slower speed than others, so handling should be adjusted according to each individual hound. A puppy who is excited and playing about may calm down if his handler walks, (as long as it is fast enough for the puppy to be trotting), instead of running, which makes the puppy think it is a game.

When you have learned the standard and have begun to apply it to the hounds in the ring, you will be able to see that it is possible to help camouflage faults by clever handling. (This should not fool a judge, of course). However, you can also draw attention to faults,

Ch. Fearnwood Skylark bred by Lesley Patrick

Ch. Hyndsight Flair bred by S. Finnett and R. Heathcote   (Photo by Carol Ann Johnson)

The show ring in 1964...

....and in 1990

unless you can do it fairly unobtrusively. Constantly pushing up a hound's stomach will make it obvious that you think he has a flat topline, for instance, whereas, if left alone, it may not have been any worse than most of the others. It is only possible to correct faults in this way when the hound is standing. As soon as he moves, everything shows up.

Movement

In order for a Deerhound to look and move at his best, he needs to be in good condition and have some muscle. If he is fit, his movement will be correspondingly tighter, and any deviation from the true line will not be so obvious.

Puppies should not have road work at a young age, and their movement is often erratic. If it is really bad, there is no point in showing them at championship shows, as the first impression is important. Open shows will give you both some practice and are not so competitive.

There are many excellent books on movement in dogs, so there is no point in going into it in great detail again here. I will just describe the most common movement faults in Deerhounds today.

Pacing is a two-time movement, where the legs on the same side move forward together, as opposed to the diagonally opposite pairs in the trot. It can be caused by regularly walking the hound at too slow a pace, so that he cannot maintain a trot, but finds it uncomfortable to walk for too long. It can also be caused by faulty construction or by pain in the back that the hound is trying to alleviate by changing the way he moves. It looks odd when viewed from the side, and even worse coming and going as it makes the hound appear to roll from side to side. In the ring, it is necessary to surprise the hound into breaking the habit, usually by setting off at a very fast pace and slowing as he breaks into a trot.

Cow-hocks are weak hock joints that turn in towards each other when viewed from the rear and are usually found with good rear angulation. They are worsened by allowing a growing hound to stand on his hind legs a lot, putting undue strain on them. They are unsightly standing and will appear even worse when the hound is moving away. Suitable exercise may strengthen them and age may correct them to some extent.

Hounds moving straight but close behind can be improved by exercise and building up the muscle in the hindquarters. This should help, but this construction is largely hereditary and care should be taken when choosing a stud dog for a bitch that is deficient in this way.

Loose elbow action is usually caused by a straight shoulder or more usually a straight upper arm that sets the elbow in front of the chest, rather than against the ribs, so it has less support. Exercise may help tighten it to some extent but it will always be there. Loose wrist action may be helped to some extent by exercise. Short or high-stepping front action, (when viewed from the side), is usually caused by too short an upper arm, which cannot be corrected, but may not look as bad when moving slowly.

All the exercise suggested in the above paragraphs as a corrective measure, should not be carried out until the hound is over a year old. Before that time it is likely to make the problem worse or may actually cause the problem in the first place.

Not a movement fault, but noticeable on the move, is a gay tail, carried above the level of the topline. It may be possible to train a hound to carry his tail lower by tapping it when practising at home, but the fault will always be there and is caused by poor hind construction. Sometimes young male Deerhounds go through a phase of carrying their tails higher than normal in the ring, trying to assert themselves. However, good tail-sets are hereditary and a hound with a correctly set tail will find it difficult to carry it above the line of the back.

Further showing

Assuming that you have been bitten by the showing bug, the next step is to join the Deerhound Club if you have not already done so, so that you will be eligible to win a variety of awards from the club. These will be listed in the literature sent out to you when you are accepted.

If you buy a weekly dog paper, you will see that it lists all the shows, so that you can obtain schedules of those that you wish to enter. There are breed notes, which give details of other events taking place, results of shows and other items of news in the Deerhound world. The paper will also print critiques written by judges from the shows that have already taken place so that, if you are lucky enough to win, you can actually find out what the judge thought of your beloved.

The first few years of showing can be the most exciting because there is so much to learn, so many people to get to know, and it can feel as if initial progress is rapid. There is a very good saying in the world of dogs that when someone has been in a breed for two years they know everything, when they have been in for five years, they know nothing! It is as well to remember this. Because it is possible to learn so much at the start, it is easy for an exhibitor to think they know a lot. However, the longer you spend learning, and the more you learn, the more you will realise there is that you still don't know. Therefore, ask as many questions as you can and listen to the answers. Or sit beside someone you respect and listen to what they have to say. Listen rather than talk at this stage. Otherwise you may look back with embarrassment on some of the things you said!

Once an exhibitor gets over their nerves and realises that showing is more than a matter of turning up, trotting up and down, standing and winning a prize, then they will begin to make progress. Hopefully it will be gradual, so that each milestone means something - the first first, the first reserve CC, the first CC, and so on.

Championship Shows

These are the main events of the show calendar, and the idea of going to them, for some people, is to win a first in certain classes to qualify for Crufts, or eventually to win a Challenge Certificate, three of which will make your Deerhound a champion. Before you get to this stage, there are still other exciting things to aim for. After the judging, you may notice that the judge appears to be judging classes that are not in the catalogue. This is because we are lucky in Deerhounds to have a lot of lovely old trophies, some of which are won on a points system over the year, the points being awarded at championship shows where CCs are on offer. These are for best type, best bred by exhibitor, best not bred by exhibitor, best of the reserve CC winners, best over five, best under two, best under three, best head and expression, best brace and best hound whose owner has never won a CC in the breed. These are all decided by the judge on the day, but there are plenty of others that you may be eligible for. There is a new members cup, for exhibitors who joined the club the year before, and many others based on points won at both open and championship shows over the year. Club silver spoons can be won for six first prizes at different championship shows. There is a book all about the various trophies, which is available from the club.

In step... Miss Hartley with Ch. Rotherwood Brandon

The Breed Show

This most prestigious occasion deserves a section of its own, as it is unique among breed shows, and covers a whole weekend. The venue changes each year to give all members a chance of attending at least occasionally, even if they do not show, and takes place in an hotel. The A.G.M. is held on the Friday afternoon, with entertainment on the Friday evening. The main show is held on the Saturday, has the biggest entry of any show, and takes all day. On the Saturday evening there is the show dinner and trophy presentation, and the trophies are really worth viewing. The show ends on Sunday with some of the more unusual classes.

Even if you do not show, do make the effort to go to at least one Breed Show, even if just on the Saturday. It is wonderful to see so many Deerhounds in one place, and you are sure to meet some of your Deerhound's relations. There are also trade stands, with various breed-related items.

Photographs

When you eventually have success in the ring, you may want to advertise the fact, or put a picture of your hound in the annuals or the Breed Show catalogue. Do make sure that the photograph is both a clear picture of the actual hound and also that he appears to be a good specimen of the breed. If not sure, ask for a second opinion. I have seen some really dreadful pictures over the years, some so memorable that other people still remember them and even which publication they were in! A lot of exhibitors keep their records indefinitely and it would be a shame if, in the future, this was exhibitors only reference of him.

Another point of view, if a sad one, is that we never know how long we are going to have our Deerhounds. Take those pictures now, just in case, while your hound is at his peak.

Telephone Bills

It is nice that there is just one national Deerhound Club, and that numbers are relatively small, because it enables everyone to know everyone. Suddenly you have friends all over the country. Be warned, however, that your phone bill will rise dramatically. Not only do Deerhound people live too far away, but can they talk!

Things not to do

The most obvious of these would be breaking Kennel Club rules. The main ones are printed in the schedules, but it is possible to obtain them in full from the Kennel Club. They do change from time to time, however, and changes are published in the Kennel Gazette. Significant changes are also published in the weekly dog papers. These rules are important and exhibitors have been disqualified for various offences.

There are other things that are not against any rules, but are not the 'done thing', such as entering the same hound under a judge who has already awarded it a CC. Exceptions would be made in the case of the Breed Show or Crufts.

Taking a bitch who is in season to a show is not a very considerate thing to do. Keeping her on the bench does not make a lot of difference, as males can smell a bitch in season over a great distance. It upsets not only the other Deerhounds on the day, (actually, knowing how laid-back they are about sex, it probably affects them the least!), but also all the other males at the show.

Upsetting, in any way, other Deerhounds or their owners in the ring, by deliberately obscuring them or interfering with them, or allowing your hound to do the same, is not very sporting. If someone does this to you, take it as a compliment - the exhibitor obviously thinks you are going to beat him!

Try not to overtake other exhibitors when moving round the ring together. If you wish to move your hound quickly, then stand at, or near, the front of the line. If you know that you cannot run very fast, then it is only fair to stand at the end of the line, or have someone else run your hound for you, rather than hold everyone up. If the exhibitor in front of you is moving too slowly, it is better to stop and give them room to get out of the way as you are doing your hound no favours if moving him too slowly.

It goes without saying that a dog that is ill should never be taken to a show. Neither should one that is nasty as, besides any moral implications, an incident at a show could result in not only the offending dog being banned for life, but also any progeny he might have. Quite apart from that, when at a show, you are on show, and owe it to your breed not to bring it into disrepute.

And last but not least, try not to complain if you don't win - not in too loud a voice, anyway - there will be lots of other shows.

Other thoughts

To start with, it is all too easy to be strongly influenced by just one person. If some sort of dispute arises, try to hear all the other points of view before you make any decision about who is right. Most situations are not black and white anyway.

Try not to confuse Deerhounds with their owners. The owner may not be your favourite person, but that does not mean that all the Deerhounds they have are rubbish. And vice versa. Nice owners do not necessarily have wonderful Deerhounds. It is sometimes difficult to separate the two at first, but gets easier with experience.

Before you strongly criticise a Deerhound that consistently beats yours, think how that makes your own hound look!

Stewarding

This is an interesting way to be involved in the show scene if you don't actually want to compete, and is a responsible and worthwhile job. Good stewards are always in short supply.

To start with it would be better to work with an experienced steward as there are a few things to remember and it is necessary to be careful and methodical. A copy of the catalogue needs to be marked, the absentees must be noted in the judging book, the results of each class must be recorded in triplicate, for the show, the Kennel Club and the ringside, the classes have to be called in at the right time, seen hounds arranged in order, prize cards sorted and handed out and refreshments organised for the judge. In breeds with small entries it helps to have two stewards, as there is not enough time during the classes to complete all the paper work. It also helps if one of the stewards has a loud voice! Once proficient, it will be possible to steward at championship shows, where it is often possible to choose which breeds you would like to steward for. A lot can be learned by sitting and watching an experienced judge going over a nice entry of any breed.

It is now a requirement of any person wishing to award CCs for the first time that they should have had three years experience of stewarding at a minimum of twelve shows.

Judging

After you have been showing for a reasonable length of time, (at least five years), hopefully with some success, it is possible that you may be asked to judge a small show. Before this time you will have to get experience from going over your own hounds, and comparing them with the standard, followed by hounds owned by friends, with whom you can exchange views. One of the best ways to learn is by comparison, and if every hound you examine has the same neck or shoulder, for instance, it is not as easy to learn to differentiate good from bad. Learn to be observant, and pay attention at shows to hounds both standing and moving. Also notice that each hound looks different from show to show. When judging, it is how the hound looks on that particular day that is important, not how much you know he has won in the past.

Do attend any breed seminars, whether judging seminars or not. Whatever stage you are at, there will always be something to learn. It is not a good enough excuse to say they are too far away - if you wish to judge, you will have to travel far and wide, and at your own expense, in order to learn anything. The more Deerhounds it is possible to go over, the better, and at these seminars, there are always some very good hounds, that you would not get the chance to go over in the normal scheme of things.

If you are lucky enough to get asked to judge, then that is when you really begin to learn. I remember how amazed I was at how hounds felt so different when I could actually get my hands on them, as I had assumed that all Deerhounds felt like my own, more or less. I still feel extremely privileged to be allowed to go over other exhibitors' hounds like this. And I still learn a lot each time.

However, can I just point out that judging is in no way compulsory. If you don't like the thought of judging, then don't judge. If it is going to give you sleepless nights, before or after, why make life difficult for yourself? Unfortunately, this is the one time in the ring when spectators really are looking at you! They will all be very quick to judge you - after all, that is one of the main subjects at the ringside at any show.

If you really want to judge, then, assuming that you are still avidly learning as much as you can all the time, it doesn't matter what criticisms are levelled at you as long as you can justify your placings. Judges often disagree - that is the whole point in showing. Judges also make mistakes and, as long as they are genuine mistakes, they are part of the learning process.

Requirements
The first requirement of any judge is that they are honest. It does not matter one iota how knowledgeable a judge is, if they don't apply that knowledge but instead place dogs for other reasons.

The next essential is that they should know the breed standard. Really they should know it off by heart. At least then, if anyone should question them about a hound, they can give a sensible answer with sound reasoning. Be happy to defend your decisions - there is no right or wrong (in most cases anyway) - all judging is subjective.

Do judge to the standard rather than handling or behaviour. When moving, as long as the exhibit takes a few strides in a straight line it is possible to assess the movement. Nor should a Deerhound have to stand like a statue in order for a judge to see type, shape or conformation. In fact, most faults are more likely to be visible when the hound is moving rather than stacked in a way that is meant to camouflage faults. Remember you are judging hounds not robots.

The only behaviour that should not be tolerated is untypical behaviour. A Deerhound should be friendly and pleasant. It would be nice if they were all outgoing but unfortunately most do not like showing all that much. A youngster may be apprehensive, but not excessively so, and never really nervous. When judging puppies and, for that matter juniors, who will not have been shown all that much, be kind and gentle and, if necessary, play with them to put them at ease. The attitude of the judge at the youngster's first few shows can have a big influence on its views of showing. Aggressive behaviour should never be tolerated, and I would expect an exhibitor to withdraw a dog the first time it happened and not to show it again. If a dog actually tries to bite a judge, and the judge dismisses it from the ring, it is now a Kennel Club requirement that the dog in question is reported.

Do judge the whole dog, and not get obsessed with one or two points. A Deerhound should be typical and it should be balanced, giving a pleasing overall picture, combining strength with quality. It should not resemble any other breed. The individual points obviously matter, but it is possible to have a majority of excellent features that are put together wrongly, and do not add up to a Deerhound.

Type is of the utmost importance. Movement matters, not least because it can emphasise virtues and show up many faults not apparent standing but, as has often been said before, a mongrel can move well. Movement should also be typical, the hound moving forward with a long effortless stride. The hindquarters should provide a lot of drive, the hocks flexing and extending. The forequarters should extend sufficiently to balance this, with a low easy stride. Short or high-stepping strides indicate faults in front assembly. Viewed from front or rear, the limbs should move in a straight line, without any deviation.

Learn to look for the virtues, rather than the faults. Anyone can find fault, but it is a much better viewpoint if you can look on the positive side.

Do write a critique afterwards. If you have time to judge, you have time to write a critique, and it is also part of the learning process. If a judge does not write a critique, I assume that they cannot justify their decisions in print, or that they are lacking in manners. The exhibitors have paid a small fortune to enter the show, with entries and petrol and so forth, and the least a judge can do is to write a few words to explain his decisions. Try to give a good description and find at least one virtue - these are your winners, after all. Also say why you preferred the winner over the second. Critiques that say more or less the same about each dog are not very interesting, so take detailed notes. It is impossible to remember exactly what you thought later. However if you really are capable of judging, then you should be more than capable of writing a critique.

Records

From the time you begin judging it is imperative to keep accurate records of all the shows, the date, number of entries and the hounds present. If you ever have to fill in a Kennel Club questionnaire when first proposed to award CCs, these records are important. If there are errors, the Kennel Club may impose a lengthy ban.

The negative side?

Learning about Deerhounds, and indeed all dogs, is very enjoyable but it does have a negative side. Now that I have learned to really look at dogs, taking in as much as possible, it is not something that I am able to switch off. These days I cannot greet a friend's retriever and give it a pat without noticing the shape of its skull or the way it moves towards me. When glancing at a mongrel in the street, I find that I am subconsciously noting the fact that it is cow-hocked and has flat feet.

I am too aware of all my Deerhounds' faults and, though it obviously doesn't stop me from loving them, I sometimes think it would be nice to see them only as the grey hairy friends their predecessors used to be many years ago.

Chapter Ten

OTHER ACTIVITIES

Coursing

There is a coursing section of the Deerhound Club, open to all paid-up members of the club, which organises meetings at which Deerhounds can course hares. While this is not their true purpose in life and will obviously not test strength and courage, it is the only way these days to test the keenness to chase, coupled with speed and agility. Even this option will probably not be available for very much longer.

Most meetings are walked-up, which means that a line of enthusiasts, accompanied by their Deerhounds advance slowly across field or moor, depending on the part of the country in which the meeting is taking place. The slipper, who has the two Deerhounds with him who are running next, walks slightly ahead of the line, and when a hare is startled into action, he makes sure both hounds are sighted on the hare and then releases them from slips. One hound wears a white collar and one a red collar, each time, and the judge, usually mounted, follows the course and holds up a white or red flag to signify to the rest of the line which hound has won. The object is not to kill the hare, but to see which hound is closest and turns it the most.

It is a knock-out competition, though if hares are plentiful there will be also be a stake for the first round losers, and possibly also the second round losers, so that everyone has a chance to run their hound more than once.

Deerhounds need to be extremely fit for coursing, (as do their owners!). Coursing is quite arduous and not a little dangerous, although fatalities are rare. The coursing in Scotland is usually on moorland and requires negotiating deep heather and boggy ground. The courses are usually shorter and most of the enthusiasts see very little of the coursing! In East Anglia the coursing is across open fields, across plough, stubble and frozen furrows, which can all be just as taxing, and in some areas there are dikes, which are hidden dangers for hounds in full flight. Courses tend to be longer, and test stamina more than agility.

There are occasionally driven meetings in which hares are actually driven towards the line of walkers, where hares are more plentiful and space is limited. This is less energetic for the walkers, and it is usually possible to see more of the actual coursing.

The most famous and prestigious of the meetings is the Dava meeting, a joint Deerhound and Saluki meeting held in November on Dava moor. The breeds run separately but the overall winners in each breed then run off against one another. It is also a great social occasion.

For more information, Kenneth Cassel's book 'A perfect creature of Heaven' is primarily about coursing.

Lure-coursing

This is coursing after an artificial hare, usually a plastic bag, though some are slightly more realistic! It is possible to buy the equipment needed to run the lure, and meetings are held in various parts of the country, often as fund-raising events. Again two hounds are slipped and the winner is the fastest. These events have not become all that popular in Britain, though if hare-coursing becomes illegal, this could be the sport of the future.

Some hounds can become over-excited at these events and may be possessive over the lure if they catch up with it. A hound that is likely to snap at another in this situation should wear a muzzle when running.

Racing

Some Greyhound tracks have one day a month when other, usually related, breeds can go and race. Hounds can be started in traps, but usually these are too small for Deerhounds and they are slipped by hand as the 'hare' goes past on the rails. Two or three usually race together and can be timed. As the track is circular, and as most Deerhounds are not stupid, many jump the rails and cut across the centre to turn the 'hare' back. This rather defeats the object, however. Some do run round just for the joy of running, but older ones often can't be bothered. It is enjoyable to watch the keen ones racing, and some are very fast.

Racing can sometimes bring out the excitable or aggressive side of a hound's character, in which case he should wear a muzzle for racing. Some tracks may insist on this.

Seminars/Teach-ins

There is usually at least one such event each year. Do make the effort to go to them if you can, even if you do not participate in competitive events. Most include something of interest to everyone, and it also gives you a chance to get to know other people who share your love of the breed, and to make friends.

Many subjects are covered, not just showing and judging, such as the history of the breed, various veterinary topics, breeding and nutrition, for instance. Sometimes it is nice just to have time to chat.

Social Events

Some members organise purely social events such as lunches, parties, fun days or simply get-togethers after shows. If there is nothing in your area, think of organising something yourself or with a friend. If everyone would take the trouble, at some point, to organise something, it would make them more tolerant of other people's efforts. And there would certainly be many more events on the calendar!

Picking winners

Ch. Sorisdale MacEithne bred by K.A.H Cassels   (Photo by Hancock)

Chapter Eleven

BREEDING

Breeding a Deerhound of your own, can be interesting, exciting and rewarding. It can also be anything from expensive and disappointing to absolutely heartbreaking. Unless you are one hundred per cent certain that you want to breed from your bitch, then don't. It is so much easier to buy a puppy you like from a breeder than to risk the life of your bitch in an experimental exercise.

Of all activities connected with dogs, breeding is the most important. It should not be undertaken by anyone who has not given it serious thought. Breeders have an enormous responsibility - to the breed, to the people who will be buying the puppies and to society as a whole, now that so many people have an anti-dog attitude. Even if you start off with the right intentions, many things can still go wrong. So if you don't think it is the most important thing you have ever done in dogs, then leave it to those who will take it seriously.

Wrong reasons for breeding

There was a time when vets used to tell pet owners that it was a good idea to have a litter from their bitch because it would prevent her from getting a pyometra later in life. However the last two pyometras that I have heard of in Deerhounds were actually in bitches who have had a litter. The only way to prevent a pyo is to have a bitch spayed.

It is not a good idea to breed for money. Your Deerhound did not ask to be born and does not owe you a living, any more than your children do. Keeping and breeding animals for profit is farming, so that anyone breeding purely for money is puppy farming, regardless of how many litters are bred. Besides, if you raise them in the right way with enough quality food and keep them until the right age to sell, your profit margin, if any, will be small.

Some pet owners want another Deerhound just like the one they have. However, without the experience to choose, how will they pick the one from the litter that is like mum? Even experienced breeders cannot predict with certainty how a puppy will turn out, so what chance has a novice? There is also no guarantee that you will even get the right sex, as it is possible to get a litter of all one sex. And if you really think so much of your bitch, why risk her life in such a gamble?

Right reasons for breeding

The only good reasons for breeding are to improve on what you have, and to benefit the breed as a whole. In order to improve on what you have, it is necessary to have a thorough knowledge of the breed and the breed standard. Unless the virtues and faults of the bitch are taken into consideration, it will not be possible to choose a suitable stud-dog.

One thing that no-one should ever attempt to correct by breeding is a bad temperament. A dog with a bad temperament should never, ever be bred from.

Breeding is difficult enough if you have some knowledge and go about it in the right way. Nothing about breeding is easy. Perhaps that is why it is such a challenge.

Before you begin

If you have decided that breeding is for you, there are yet more considerations before you put any plans into progress.

The most important is time. To raise a litter properly, it will take a large part of every day for approximately three months. This is for the basic feeding, cleaning up, washing bedding and so on. (For a week of this, around whelping time, almost twenty-four hour care will be needed). If watching the puppies is included it will take most of each day. If you work part-time, it will be necessary to arrange holiday at this time. If you work full-time, it shouldn't be contemplated without employing someone else to do the work for you.

Another consideration is money. Besides the stud-fee, bedding and whelping-box, there is the cost of feeding the puppies. From the age of ten weeks to the age of around fifteen months, a puppy will cost considerably more to feed than an adult. Imagine the food bill if you don't find homes for your puppies by the time they are ready to go. Do you have homes lined up for the puppies? Good homes are difficult to find.

There needs to be a quiet room in the house or elsewhere, where the bitch can have her puppies and feel secure. This may mean rearranging the house for a while. When the puppies are three or four weeks old, they will need a larger area in which to play, preferably an outside run, so that they can get some fresh air.

Time of year

It used to be rule of thumb that one did not mate a bitch before the shortest day of the year or after the longest one. The reasoning behind this was that puppies born September onwards would be growing up in the winter, when they would need more expensive heating and that they would not have suitable weather in which to play out.

This is not so important these days as more puppies are born in the house, which is probably heated anyway, although they will need some heat once they are weaned or they will use up much of their food just keeping warm. Although puppies are easy to manage in the house until they are around four weeks, after that, if there are more than a couple of puppies, the family might have to move out. (In fact, they would probably want to move out). However, outside in winter, puppies will spend a lot of their playing time cold and wet, which is not conducive to optimum growth.

It is largely a matter of the facilities available, and the more you plan carefully, the easier it will be when the puppies arrive. Puppies born February onwards will be growing up as the weather becomes better and will be able to play in the sunshine.

One consideration for whelping in the winter months is that some bitches can get too hot when nursing a litter in summer. A bitch of mine who whelped in July would not have any bedding in the box and just scratched it out of the way, so that in the end I had to remove it so that the puppies didn't get scratched up along with the bedding. Unfortunately because mum was then lying on bare boards she developed a pressure sore which didn't clear until the puppies were a few weeks old and didn't need her constant presence. Having said that, my last puppies were born at the end of October and, although they were in the house, I couldn't put a heat lamp or even any heating in the room or mum behaved in exactly the same way and was obviously too hot, even though the room seemed cold to me when I was sitting with them. The puppies did not mind and usually lay away from her so were not feeling cold. This is a good example of how mother knows best. Deerhounds vary, as do people, and it is best not to try to impose your own will too much in these situations.

Age

The earliest I know of a normal Deerhound bitch coming into season is eight months and the latest is twenty-three months, and both bitches went on to have normal seasons. (I have heard of a bitch coming in season later than this but she then came in season sporadically and did not ever produce puppies). Most have their first season at between ten and fourteen months and then every six to eight months.

Deerhounds are slow-maturing and it is not wise to mate them too early in life, certainly not much before they are two, at the earliest, and not before their second season, preferably later. At the other end of the scale, a bitch is generally too old to have a first litter over the age of six. Common sense should prevail, and obviously some bitches are much fitter than others of a similar age.

Aims

The first thing to decide is what you are aiming for. Surprisingly this is not something one hears mentioned all that often. When discussing breeding, people say what they want to correct, or discuss the faults and virtues of various stud-dogs, (usually faults). It is apparent, when looking at Deerhounds as opposed to many other breeds, that most breeders are not actually aiming for anything in particular whereas, in the past, it was much easier to tell from which kennel a certain hound had originated.

All Deerhounds should be typical of their breed, but in this section I am using the word 'type' in the way it is most often used, that is to denote a certain sort of look.

Before embarking on breeding, it is necessary to have in mind the type you want to produce, and the particular virtues that are the most important to you. (These may vary, but only slightly, from litter to litter according to the bitch, or if you find you have made a mistake, but the overall look should be the same). Because of this, I do not think it is possible to breed good Deerhounds without knowing the breed standard and also looking at a lot of Deerhounds every year, not just the first time you breed. Really the only way to do this is to go to shows, where there is a good selection from which to make comparisons. If the only Deerhounds you see are your own, it is easy to think that all Deerhounds look like that and, by breeding, to eventually get away from the typical Deerhound. It has been done!

The show-ring is the serious breeders' yardstick, by which they can see how their Deerhounds compare with others, and to be able to see the best in the country at any one time. Deerhounds look different at home. It is necessary to compare them at the same time in the same place.

Remember that exaggeration is not enhancement. A dark eye is good, for example, but a black eye is not better. Do not breed from a fault just because you happen to like it or think it looks eye-catching - examples might be an over-long neck or very short coat. Showing Deerhounds like this encourages others to do the same. Breeders must breed to the standard and not change the Deerhound by ignorance or arrogance. If the correct Deerhound is not to your liking, then try a different breed.

Of course it is possible to physically breed a litter without knowledge of the standard and without going to shows to learn and to see if you got it right, and even produce something decent by chance. But it is not possible to breed something of excellence that will go on to produce other excellent specimens. For a smaller outlay, fewer risks and considerably greater returns, it would be better to put the money on the lottery.

It costs the same to do it wrong as to do it right. Take the trouble to breed a litter of which you can be justifiably proud.

Choosing a stud-dog

If this is your first litter, it is best to discuss this with your bitch's breeder, who should have more experience and be able to offer advice, but will hopefully take into account any strong ideas of your own.

The most important consideration is temperament. Do not use a dog whose temperament is in the least suspect, however attractive his appearance. You may be able to cope with such a temperament, but most of the puppies you produce will go to pet homes and these people may not know how to cope. And even if they do, why should they have to? (And please, no excuses about upbringing or other dogs picking on him).

It is necessary to know the strengths and failings of your bitch and to try to improve on the failings without losing the strengths, more easily said than done. If you do not have much experience yet, it may be best to use a dog who is winning consistently, in good company at championship shows. It does not necessarily have to be the top winner, rather choose the one whose pedigree complements that of your bitch, and whose type you like. If your bitch is line-bred, try to choose a dog of similar breeding. If she is very closely bred, it may be better to use a dog only slightly or not related, in the next generation, and then breed back to that line. However, in Deerhounds, not many are line-bred, in which case choose a line you like from the pedigree and breed to that.

If you like a fairly close relation in the pedigree, this could prove a successful mating and a good basis for future line-breeding. The most common matings of this kind are grand-parent to grand-child, uncle to niece or aunt to nephew. If a half-brother to half-sister mating is considered, the parent in common should be a champion or an acknowledged, excellent specimen of the breed, as he or she will have considerable influence. Also, if breeding closely, it is even more important that both prospective parents do not exhibit the same faults.

Try to get your priorities right. Choose the right dog, no matter where he lives. It is hard to understand why some people will travel the length and breadth of the country to show, but can't be bothered to travel very far for a stud-dog. Breeding requires a great deal more thought and responsibility than showing and should be treated accordingly.

It is best not to breed from a second generation fault or double up on a fault. To those in their second, or more, generation of breeding it is good advice not to breed from a bitch who is not as good as her mother. It makes more sense to have a second litter from the mother instead.

As Deerhounds are not always keen stud-dogs, it may be that the chosen dog may not mate your bitch. Sometimes the litter brother can be used instead, but only if he is equally good, not just for the sake of it. It is probably better to use the stud-dog's father.

Unless you have a lot of experience, it is better to use a dog whose progeny you have already seen and liked, rather than a young dog. In any case, it is better not to use a maiden dog on a maiden bitch, especially if the owners are also inexperienced.

Once you have chosen your dog, ask the stud-dog owners if they are agreeable and find out the stud-fee. It is best to pay a straight fee rather than give a puppy in lieu. If the fee is a puppy, every eventuality should be covered - single puppies for instance - as many disagreements have ensued from this sort of arrangement. If the dog is not yet proven, usually the fee is much less, or is delayed until the bitch is in whelp. Whatever the arrangements between you, write everything down. It is very easy to forget what each party has said.

If you have chosen the stud-dog with care, and he is definitely the right one, and you do not get a mating, the obvious thing to do is to wait until the next season. If the dog is right, then there is no point in going to another one. If he isn't the right one, then why go to him at all? At the second attempt, it may be as well to have another one in reserve, just in case, but at least you will have had time to give it as much thought as your first choice. To go from dog to dog, especially of different types, trying to get a mating at all costs, smacks of desperation rather than dedication.

Mating

There is one simple rule that will go further to ensuring a good mating than probably any other. Take the bitch to the stud-dog on the day that is right for the bitch, not the day that is right for you! It is amazing how many bitches are 'ready' on a Sunday. I sometimes wonder if that is why some stud-dogs are not as keen as they might be. Even some experienced stud-dogs will only mate a bitch on the one day she is ready and no other. Therefore, if you miss this day, you are not going to get a successful mating. (It may also be worth bearing in mind that if you mate your bitch on a Saturday or a Sunday, she will probably whelp at a weekend too, which means more expensive vet bills if anything goes wrong!).

The bitch should be in good condition and fit, but not fat. Bitches are usually ready to mate around the thirteenth to sixteenth day of their season, though anything from the tenth to the seventeenth day is common enough. One does sometimes hear of bitches who have been mated very early in a season, but it could be that the earlier part of the season has gone unnoticed. However, bitches do vary a lot, and also vary from season to season, so just because she appeared to be ready on a certain day last season does not mean it will be the same this season. I think it more likely that you will get a good mating slightly late in the season than slightly early, so do not panic and arrive too early, and then wonder why the dog isn't interested.

Throughout the season, bitches have a discharge. Usually it is some shade of red to start with, becoming gradually paler around the tenth day until, by the time she is ready to mate, it is straw-coloured. (However some retain the colour all season, regardless of mating, and some never have much colour at all). At the same time, the vulva swells and softens. If you have other bitches, they may mount each other from around the tenth day, not necessarily when ready for mating, just practising. If you also have dogs, it is not a good idea to let them practise at any time after she has started the season! Apart from colour and softening, another way to tell when she is ready, is to stroke along the back and croup and she will turn her tail. At first it will just move to the side, but when ready, she will kink it sideways at the top and the vulva will twitch upwards. The skin along the back may also ripple.

As soon as the bitch is in season, inform the stud-dog owner, and also make arrangements to stay overnight, either with them if they offer, or nearby. It may be that you will not get a mating right away, especially if you are being too anxious and have arrived too early in the season. If you are going to breed, don't do it half-heartedly! Do stay until you have a mating, don't rush off after a couple of hours because you have other things to do. Quite a lot of owners do this, and it seems pointless. The dog will mate the bitch when she is ready. Sometimes the bitch is apprehensive and it may settle her if there is somewhere safe that she and the dog can play together and get to know each other. There should always be someone available to hold the bitch if the dog mounts her as twisting at the wrong time may injure the dog, or put him off.

However if the bitch is obviously ready and the dog is inexperienced, or can't quite get it right, and needs some encouragement, it may help to pretend to take the bitch away. He will be all the keener when she reappears. Running her away from him, on a lead, will also stir him into action. Some stud-dogs are better if one or both of the owners are not present, especially if the dog has been discouraged from taking an interest in the opposite sex. Some even need lifting on the right end, but then seem to get the hang of it. Others are at the opposite extreme and these are harder to handle as they are so eager that they can frighten the bitch. On the other hand, if the dog is not interested, you will not get a mating. If the bitch isn't interested, she can be encouraged. There is a difference, however, between encouragement and complete restraint, and any bitch who has to be tied down or held by three people, may have a reason of her own for not breeding. If it is known that the bitch has some sort of problem, with temperament or construction, which may hinder whelping and that she may pass on to her offspring, it is not doing either them or the breed any favours to breed from her. It is unnecessary and possibly harmful.

The stud fee is for the service of the stud-dog, and is payable whether or not there are any puppies from the mating. If there is a good mating and the bitch misses it is usual, though not compulsory, for the bitch to get a free return, but this needs to be agreed in advance. Some people like a second mating. This may be advisable with a maiden dog, but is otherwise unnecessary, and can make estimating the date of whelping more difficult.

Bitches may miss because they are mated on the wrong day, or because they have an infection. If the bitch has missed, it may be as well to have her checked before a second mating, to make sure everything is all right. Some stud-dog owners may insist on this as the infection could be passed on to the dog, and then to any other bitches who visit him.

The stud-dog owner

Owning a stud-dog carries as much responsibility as breeding from a bitch. It should not be seen as an easy way of making some money, by allowing all and sundry to use him.

The stud-dog owner has almost equal responsibility with the breeder. If at any time in the future any of the offspring are in need of assistance and the breeder, for whatever reason, is unable to help, it is then up to the stud-dog owner to do what they can. These Deerhounds are half the dog's breeding.

When accepting a bitch, as much care should be taken as when choosing a dog, and one also needs to check whether the owner of the bitch has the facilities and knowledge to take care of the bitch throughout this time and be sure that they will raise the puppies with care and find them decent homes.

Pregnancy

Bitches should be treated as normal after mating, they are not ill. However stress can prevent conception and the bitch's routine should be as normal. Any bitch who is very attached to her owner should really not be left in kennels or otherwise have her routine disrupted if at all possible, for any time during her pregnancy.

About two to three weeks after mating is a crucial time, when the embryos are implanting into the wall of the uterus. At this time bitches may lose their appetite, (as they can do when not mated). The hormonal changes take place in the body whether mated or not. If the bitch is fit and healthy, there is no need to worry, as she will usually resume eating normally at around five or six weeks. Occasionally a bitch will not eat well for the whole of her pregnancy, which can be a worry, though does not seem to affect the puppies. If she gets to seven weeks and will not eat, then give her anything that will encourage her, of some nutritional value, that is. Yorkshire pudding, rice pudding, rice, pasta, bread and butter, home-made cake or digestive biscuits will usually tempt even the most stubborn, and obviously any sort of meat or dog food.

If pregnant, there is no need to increase the food intake until the seventh week, and then only slightly - it is the quality that should be increased rather than the quantity. Too much food may make the bitch fat, or the puppies too big, both of which will make for a more difficult whelping. It is not necessary to feed extra calcium, and in fact this may be harmful and bring the possibility of eclampsia. If calcium is given, it should be in association with vitamin D and given after whelping.

About three to four weeks after mating, the nipples may look a little pinker, and from then on will grow slightly and eventually may lose the surrounding hair. At around five weeks there is usually a slight thickening along the bitch's flanks, and if it is a large or a second litter it is apparent that the bitch is in whelp. With a first litter, it may not be obvious until six or seven weeks. If there are no symptoms by the eighth week, she probably isn't expecting, unless she has just a single pup, as these are sometimes many days overdue. The only way to be absolutely sure is to have the bitch x-rayed, but only after the due date. Bitches are often more loving after a season anyway but she may also have a different expression and may gaze at her owner as if deep in thought.

If you are impatient to know, some vets can feel puppies at four weeks. It is also possible to have the bitch scanned, but be sure to go to someone with a lot of experience as not all scanners are accurate.

The bitch can have normal exercise until she herself chooses to slow down, but it is a good idea to stop her being too energetic, or jumping. Most become more careful by choice.

Whelping preparations
The bitch must have a safe and secure place in which to whelp. This usually means a whelping box, designed for the purpose. These days it is possible to buy a ready-made one, moulded in plastic or something similar. I haven't actually seen one but they sound a good idea and would be easy to clean and sterilise between litters.

Most people make their own, although new timber would probably cost as much. The box should just be big enough for the bitch to lie on her side, approximately three and a half feet square (1.1 m), or slightly larger for a big bitch. Most do not use all the room and if too big, the puppies lose their mother when tiny and crawl round trying to find her. If

Days before whelping

Ch. Rosslyn Antic bred by Bryan Doak

Brylach Jasmine bred by C.W & M.G Spence

they get separated, the bitch becomes very anxious, and forgets the main group of puppies in her panic that one is getting lost. Timber should be varnished, so that it is less absorbent and easier to clean.

Some owners like to have pig rails round the box to help prevent the bitch from squashing the puppies against the side, or lying on them. This only applies to tiny puppies. When the pups are over ten days, and beginning to sit up, the rails should be removed as the puppies could just as easily be crushed against the rails.

If the puppies are going to live in the box for a few weeks, it is best to have one side of the box hinged at the bottom, so that the side can be dropped down and provide a ramp for them to get in and out of the box, to prevent them jolting their legs. In this case, the floor of the box should be no more than two inches off the ground or the ramp will be too steep. With a box like this, the puppies can be shut in or out of the box to facilitate cleaning, and also get in and out of the box with ease.

The best sort of bedding is vet-bed or similar man-made fur bedding, which is easy to wash and dry, and will not suffocate the puppies if they get buried in it. A few layers of newspaper underneath will absorb any fluid that passes through, leaving the surface of the bed dry. This sort of bedding is much cheaper to buy by the roll, as you will need a lot of it.

If whelping in the house, a warm room is usually enough to keep the family happy, but if the litter will be in an unheated room, it is as well to have a heat-lamp which can be suspended over the box, to provide constant heat, especially when the bitch is away from the puppies, and certainly after weaning. It is difficult to know the best height for the lamp, and it is best to be guided by the mother. She should be able to stand under it, and to get into the box without catching it, but it should be low enough to keep the bed warm. After weaning the lamp can be lower, unless the pups always lie away from it, in which case they are obviously too warm. The lamp must be secure so that it will stand up to being knocked and will not fall onto the bed where it could start a fire. Much of this is common sense.

It is a good idea to have the first aid kit handy, as you will need the thermometer at least. You will also need the vet's telephone number, just in case, and a good detailed book on whelping.

Lastly, and by far the most important thing, the bitch should be allowed to whelp where she wants to, within reason, and the box situated accordingly. If this is likely to cause problems, she should be put into her whelping quarters at least two weeks in advance, preferably before. Remove any other dogs from this room, and keep family activity to a minimum. If the bitch is not happy, she will be apprehensive about whelping which may even delay it. At the very least, she will be anxious and unhappy at the very time she should feel relaxed and secure.

Whelping

The best advice is to buy a good book on whelping. The one I usually read is 'Dogs and how to breed them' by Hilary Harmar. This deals with all the things you would want to know about dogs in general. The following are just some observations on Deerhounds in particular.

The best indication of when a bitch will whelp seems to be her temperature. Start taking this well in advance so that you know what is normal for her, and take it at the same time of day, last thing at night is best and possibly morning as well nearer the time. The normal gestation period is sixty-three days, but I think I have only had two that whelped to the day. This may be more to do with the time of mating. Healthy sperm can live for a while in the bitch but fertilisation will take place at the right time, so a bitch who is mated early may appear to be whelping late, but isn't. Large litters seem to arrive early, and small ones late but there are exceptions, of course. There are no hard and fast rules. If the temperature is normal and there is no unusual discharge don't worry. I have heard of bitches with small litters whelp almost a week late, though this is fairly uncommon.

Some bitches make beds or dig holes in the garden, (more than usual!), two or three days before they are due, but some don't and in any case it is not the performance seen in some other breeds. She may have milk for up to two days beforehand, or may not have any until after the birth of the first puppy.

Once the temperature has dropped to 99 degrees, she will probably whelp during the next twenty-four hours, and constant supervision is necessary in case she begins straining and nothing happens.

The first stage of labour, where the bitch looks uncomfortable and may pant, can happen for an hour or up to twenty-four hours, on and off, before second stage labour begins, when the bitch pants, is in discomfort and much more restless. Have a note-book and pen ready to note when you see the first real contraction. If she does not produce a puppy within two hours, it is better to ring the vet. After the first puppy, straining for more than an hour with further puppies may require veterinary assistance. If all goes well and the puppy is on its way, a maiden bitch may become agitated with a first puppy, as she is not quite sure what is happening. It is important that the owner keeps totally calm and reassures her, treating it as matter-of-factly as possible. If the owner gets agitated too, the bitch will get upset. Only if she is rushing round the box with the puppy partly out is there any need to interfere. Most bitches are very sensible. When the puppy arrives, clear the membranes from the nose and mouh and make sure he is breathing. Rubbing him with a dry towel will stimulate him to breathe and cry. Usually the bitch takes over and bites off the umbilical cord close to the body. She will probably keep pulling at it and licking the puppy furiously until you are worried that she will damage it. This is perfectly normal and you will just have to hope that the next puppy arrives fairly quickly to distract her. Some puppies head for the nipples right away and begin sucking. Others seem disinterested and even if put on do not suck for long. Sometimes squeezing out a little milk will encourage it.

Make a note of the time each puppy is born, in case it is necessary to summon the vet. I also make a note of the birth weights and all white markings so that I can identify the puppies later, when weighing them each week.

If you are at all worried about anything, telephone the vet. It is much better to be safe than sorry. Any signs of distress or unusual discharge need to be reported right away.

The bitch can go anything from ten minutes to four hours between puppies, depending on how laid-back she is and the size of the litter, but if you are sure there are more puppies and she is settling down, it may be best to ring the vet. Some bitches need an injection to start things moving again, though usually the car journey to the vet's is enough. If she wants to go outside during all this, go with her with a torch, (it's usually the middle of the night), because puppies are sometimes born outside. If not, they are born soon after the mother comes in again. Check that there is an afterbirth for each puppy, as a retained one can cause problems. You may have to be quick as the bitch will gobble them down immediately.

Once she appears settled, and has roughly the number you were expecting, have a feel each side of her stomach where she used to fat, to see if you can detect any more puppies. Usually the bitch feels quite empty when she has finished. Some people like to have the vet check her over anyway, to be on the safe side. Some give antibiotics, but this is usually unnecessary and can upset the puppies. If the bitch has to have antibiotics for any reason, it is an idea to give the puppies some plain live yoghurt to restore the balance of helpful bacteria in the digestive tract, (and mum might like it too).

Sometimes a bitch will have complete inertia, may become tired and have ineffectual contractions or will not complete natural whelping due to an exceptionally big puppy getting stuck and holding up the others. In this case she will need a caesarean section quickly or the puppies may die. Occasionally a puppy may get stuck part of the way out, often if it is a breach birth. It is possible to help it out by pulling firmly but gently in a slightly downward direction as the bitch pushes. Puppies are very slippery and it is easier to hold them with a thin towel or some kitchen roll.

When she has settled down with her family, check that she has milk and that the puppies are all sucking. Clean newspaper and bedding can be put in the box. During whelping she can be offered water regularly but will not need any food until she has finished. If she has eaten a large number of afterbirths, she will probably have diarrhoea for a day or so, but will not come to any harm. Any food should be light and easily digestible for the first couple of days before gradually building up to her normal rations by about six days, being guided by the bitch, in more frequent meals than usual as the quantity increases. She will need plenty of liquids. She will also have a discharge for at least a week. This is nothing to worry about as long as she is well in herself and it is not heavy or foul-smelling.

Culling

Not so long ago it was usual for responsible breeders to cull large litters down to six or eight puppies. A large litter is hard on the bitch, even if the puppies are rotated, and not such a good start for the puppies. There is always a big difference in the appearance of a litter of six with a comparable litter of ten or twelve. It is also not beneficial to the breed to have so many dogs with identical breeding and it is much better to have two litters of six, with different breeding, than a litter of twelve.

Sometimes very young puppies can die, or the bitch may reject or lie on one, but she is more likely to lie on one if there are twelve than if there are six, and she may well lie on a big healthy one in her efforts to avoid the three weaker ones. If puppies are weak or rejected, these are the ones to cull, because there will be a reason for this, and keeping alive at all costs puppies who have an obvious weakness is probably one of the reasons that various hereditary or congenital diseases or malformations are now more prevalent. It is also unfair on prospective purchasers, who deserve the healthiest puppies you can produce, and the breed when poorer specimens are bred from in the future.

The usual is to cull the smallest or weakest, followed by any with too much white, and this is usually done at anything up to a week after the birth. Most vets will do this with a simple injection for very little cost. It is not an easy thing to do but the bitch is more important than the puppies. Some bitch lines seem to produce smaller litters and, if you do not like the idea of culling, buy a bitch from one of these lines as it does seem to run in families.

Very few people who keep large litters, (for whatever reason they give), would do so if puppies were given away rather than sold.

Lactation

This is the hardest time for the bitch and she needs plenty of good quality food. Her intake should be increased gradually until, by the time the puppies are three weeks old, she may be eating as much as three and a half times her normal amount, with a normal size of litter, and this will continue until the puppies are fully weaned. Some don't eat quite so much and the puppies seem to thrive just as well. Leave it to the bitch to decide, she should have as much as she will eat, and plenty of liquids.

From time to time during the first few days, check that the bitch has enough milk. The puppies should feed frequently but may soon fall asleep again if they have enough milk to drink their fill quickly. Fat, sleepy contented puppies are a joy to behold, and by the time they are a day old, they should be sleek and shiny and look heavier than at birth, and then look heavier each day. If they seem thin or are crying for any length of time, there is something wrong.

Most owners will stay virtually full-time with their bitch for the first few days, sleeping in the same room. Some bitches are much more careful than others, but some are so anxious to do everything right that they panic when getting back into the box, unless the owner is there to keep all the puppies in one place while they settle down. Most bitches lick the puppies clean regularly, but if you have a bitch that is disinterested in this, it will be necessary to stimulate the puppies into passing waste by rubbing or massaging gently with a tissue or something similar, and then wiping them dry.

The puppies nails grow quickly and I like to cut them every week or so, as otherwise they scratch their mother quite badly. I use ordinary nail scissors and then a nail file to smooth them.

Weaning

If a bitch has a lot of milk, the puppies will not be very interested in other food until they are at least three weeks old. If the bitch is not feeding them well, it could be a lot earlier. I had one bitch who whelped easily but never liked the puppies much and was thoroughly fed up with them by the time they were about ten days old. They were fully weaned by the time they were two weeks old. (Her daughter, by the way, was very maternal). Nor did it set them back, they were some of the biggest pups, then biggest adults, I ever had.

Some breeders still like to feed a very mixed diet of minced beef or other meat, puppy meal, milk and eggs, which looks more appetising to humans but is much more trouble and it is hard to tell if the puppies are getting enough of the right vitamins in the right proportions. Calcium and vitamin supplements will be necessary.

A good quality complete puppy food is ideal because the manufacturers have done all the research and you know the diet will be balanced and require no additives. Everything needed for growing puppies will be there and it is best not to add meat or anything else. For puppies it is essential to feed the best quality food available. This is not the time to economise.

Puppies need just a taste to start with, a few times a day, as they will paddle in it and spread it around rather than eat it. Once they actually begin to eat, feed as much as they will clear up immediately four times a day, increasing to appetite. They should also have clean water available from this time and will eventually learn what it is for.

The bitch knows best when to stop feeding her family and bitches vary enormously. Some still want to be with the puppies at eight weeks or more, though probably more to keep an eye on them than to feed them. Once the puppies have stopped feeding, the bitch will regain her figure quickly but may be out of coat for a few months. As the puppies get older she will eat gradually less until she is back to her normal amount.

Choosing puppies

Puppies are great time-wasters! Trying to decide which puppy or puppies to keep occupies many hours of a breeder's life. If the puppy is to live in the house, then maybe just one will be kept, but by the time you have reached the stage of breeding, it is more likely that you will decide to run two on, either to delay the decision or to keep the two indefinitely.

Two puppies will keep each other company and exercise each other in the right way, playing or resting as the mood takes them. Unless you have an aversion to males, a dog and a bitch seems to be a better combination than two bitches. In my experience, bitches together do not seem to rest as much and play very rough games, compared to a dog and bitch combination.

If you are lucky, one or two puppies may really stand out in the litter and this makes it much easier to choose. Usually, however, the various good points are on different puppies. This is where it is useful to know what you are ultimately aiming for and choose the puppy who exhibits these points. In theory, the proportion of a puppy at eight weeks will be the same at eight months and at eight years. Certainly between eight and nine weeks, the puppies seem easier to assess. Before that their legs haven't grown enough, and after that they have grown too much. It is also possible to see movement at this age and the puppy should move true. One who moves well can still be ruined by incorrect exercise, but one who moves badly may never improve. Also a puppy who moves well will probably be well-constructed. A natural trot is supposed to be an indication of soundness, because it is a difficult movement for a puppy to co-ordinate. Most puppies bound everywhere.

Other breeders will usually be more than happy to come and look at your puppies though may not want to commit themselves to choose one for you. If they all choose the same one, however, the chances are that this should be at least one of the ones you keep. Occasionally a puppy will stand out because it is the biggest or the only brindle one, and various friends, doggy or not, will make a big fuss of him. That is why it is necessary to try to be objective and look at the various points and the movement as well as the overall appearance. Because you are living with them, temperament may also be an influence.

Registration
If you wish to have an affix, it is necessary to apply for one as soon as you decide to mate your bitch because it can take months to obtain one. After that it is necessary to pay an annual maintenance fee.

Once you have decided on names, it is best to send off the form to the Kennel Club as soon as possible, because it takes some time to process, especially if any of the names are refused. Do look at the sort of names that Deerhounds are usually given, or used to be given, as there are some very odd names starting to creep into the breed! As you are naming your own puppies rather than buying one that someone else has named, why not register them with the name you are actually going to call them which, in many cases, is nicer than the registered name anyway. Deerhounds don't need the long fancy names found in some other breeds, thank goodness. Short names are definitely easier when it comes to filling in entry forms. Gaelic names are fine, as long as you have checked the meaning! It is also a great help to breed enthusiasts if puppies from one litter all begin with the same letter. It makes it so much easier when doing research, or if one has a failing memory.

Worming
The puppies will need worming at approximately three, six and nine weeks, with a preparation suitable for puppies, obtainable from your vet.

Liver shunt testing
Liver shunt, or portosystemic shunt, causes great distress for both the dog and its owner. From any point of view it makes sense to have all your puppies blood tested for this at about seven weeks, or once they are fully weaned. Most vets will do this, but some have more experience of it than others, and methods and prices vary enormously for the same test. You owe it purchasers of your puppies to do all you can to ensure they get healthy pups.

It is rare for a puppy to test positive but if so, the puppy should be put down or kept by the breeder. It should not be sold.

Vaccinations
It will depend on the age the puppies are sold as to whether or not to vaccinate them. If some are unsold when you have your own puppies vaccinated, they would need to be done at the same time, as a puppy who has been vaccinated with a live vaccine may shed virus and therefore unvaccinated puppies could, in theory, catch the disease.

Selling puppies
Homes are not hard to find, but good homes are very difficult and trying to find even four or five at the same time is worse still. I would imagine finding twice as many is well nigh impossible, and yet this is one time when compromises should not be made. A breeder is responsible for these puppies all their life.

It is generally accepted that a puppy settles into a new home best between the ages of eight and twelve weeks, but it helps their development if an experienced breeder feeds and raises them, and they can play with litter-mates for as long as possible, so the usual age for letting puppies go to their new owners is at ten or eleven weeks. However, older Deerhound puppies do seem to settle down all right, usually because they relish all the extra attention.

It would be nice if they all went to live in a large house with lots of furniture to chew, had a large garden in which to dig holes and a large field of their own in which to run. Unfortunately, not many people these days have these facilities, and it is really more the attitude of mind of the prospective owner that matters, as long as they are aware that the fewer facilities they have, the more time and effort will be required. In fact, one often finds that dogs who don't have anywhere of their own in which to run get taken for more and longer walks, and may live a more interesting life than those who live in the country and are just let out to play on their own land. However, if someone is buying a puppy they should at least have a garden in which it can play. Someone without a garden would be better advised to buy an older hound.

When you get telephone enquiries, do ask the name and number of the person calling. Some people ask all sorts of questions, and then you find that they have withheld their telephone number, which makes me suspicious.

It is important to meet the prospective purchasers before they arrive to collect the puppy, as if you do not think them suitable, it is easier to say no. If they have children, it is a good opportunity to see how they treat all the dogs. Also if people have well-behaved children, they tend to have well-behaved dogs, as they will bring them up in much the same way! If they have other dogs and have brought them to visit, their temperament and condition are a good indication of their upbringing.

A sales contract would be a good idea, but it is difficult to find one that would cover all eventualities. If selling a bitch on breeding terms, or with any sale that is not straight forward, it is imperative to get everything down in writing.

Some breeders subject any prospective puppy-owners to an onslaught from all the adult Deerhounds when they arrive. Deerhounds are such friendly creatures that they love visitors far too much, and want to hug and kiss them face to face. If the visitors can enjoy this sort of treatment, they can't be all that bad, though it is a bit tough on anyone dressed to meet what they thought was a noble or docile breed. And it does get them used to the size of the breed in one quick lesson.

After-sales service

As stated before, a breeder is responsible for all the puppies they produce. You should give every new owner an information sheet and make it clear to them that they can ring if they ever have a problem, and that you will take the puppy back if they are unable to keep it for any reason. Most breeders want to do this anyway.

It is always nice when new owners keep in touch and are obviously pleased with their Deerhound. There are unexpected telephone calls, occasional visits and Christmas cards arrive with news and photographs. It makes all the hard work and soul-searching worth while.

Ch. Aviva Silver Sugi bred by Leonie Reilly

Ch. Wildtor Bodicea bred by Miss M. Gomm

Ch. Pyefleet Elspeth bred by Miss M. J. Girling

Ch. Fingon Fidranahaven bred by Dr M.G.M. McKinnon   (Photo by David Lindsay)

Chapter Twelve

HEALTH

This chapter is not meant as a substitute for veterinary advice, but more as an indication of the sort of problems you may come across with your Deerhound. There are many good veterinary books on the market, which will explain things in far greater detail. Hopefully any problems you do encounter will be mild and easily solved.

If you have a vet whom you like, and who has experience of sight-hounds, with all their idiosyncrasies, then you are extremely fortunate. When your Deerhound is ill, it can be a traumatic time and trust in your vet is essential. I am told that greyhound vets are excellent, having specialist knowledge of treatment of injuries and a practical outlook, but I have never been lucky enough to find one. However, some conditions require immediate veterinary assistance and this needs to be taken into account if choosing a vet some distance away.

If you are seriously worried about your Deerhound, its breeder is often the best person to talk to. While it is obviously unwise to make a definite diagnosis over the phone, some problems may be fairly common and you can get the advice and reassurance you need. Any breeder should be interested in your problems and willing to help, and many problems can be sorted out with a chat and common sense based on experience. This is one of the reasons for buying from a reputable and experienced breeder.

It is a good idea to have a first aid box and to update it from time to time with things you may need. Suggested items would be a thermometer, dressings, bandages, elastoplast tape, aspirin, antihistamine tablets and cream, Epsom salts, washing soda, antiseptic cream or powder, kaolin and morphine mixture, round-ended scissors, plastic syringes, vaseline, disposable gloves.

The normal temperature for a dog is 101.5 degrees Fahrenheit (approximately 38.5 degrees Celsius). His gums and the membranes inside the eye-lids should be pale pink. Very pale or deep pink gums or membranes are an indication that the hound is ill and are the first things to check if he looks unwell one day. If these do not appear normal, then take his temperature by inserting a thermometer into his rectum. (This will be easier if it is lubricated with vaseline or mild liquid soap, and I find it easier to do if the hound is lying down, as he is less likely to fidget).

If the temperature is raised then other symptoms should be noted, diarrhoea or vomiting, for instance. If the hound looks very sorry for himself, or if the temperature is over 103 degrees, or below 100 degrees, (unless whelping), then veterinary assistance should be sought. The best indication that something is wrong is a hound acting out of character, and an observant owner will often know their hound is ill before there are any symptoms.

The greatest help to any dog is an owner who is aware of any changes in his behaviour. Some people are naturally in tune with their animals which can save vital time, but any owner, with care and application, can learn by observation of their hounds in all situations.

General Veterinary Care

Deerhounds are more susceptible than some breeds to certain types of antibiotics. The trimethoprim-sulfonamide combinations are manufactured under various brand names, and have been known to have a low margin of safety in some breeds. There are also others that cause reactions and your vet, and possibly your breeder, ought to be up to date on the latest findings, as new drugs are coming onto the market all the time. Obviously hounds vary and what suits one may not suit another, but it is as well to be aware of the dangers and have your hound's veterinary records marked accordingly.

Sighthounds, in general, are not easy to anaesthetise safely, so it is best to avoid anaesthetics unless absolutely necessary. It is imperative that your vet knows the weight of your hound beforehand as many Deerhounds are not as heavy as they look, and require relatively less anaesthetic than breeds of similar weight but different type.

Many vets insist on keeping a dog in the surgery overnight to keep an eye on it. Unless the hound is seriously ill, on maintenance treatment that is impossible at home or you know that there is actually someone present in the surgery all night, personally I feel that a Deerhound will recover more quickly at home where you are available to sit up with him all night if necessary, to give him individual and loving attention in familiar surroundings.

Bloat/Distension/Torsion

This is the one occasion when there is no time to ring anyone other than the vet. If you suspect your Deerhound is starting with bloat, he needs to get to the vet immediately if not sooner. Early warning signs are the hound appearing uncomfortable, stretching, looking round at his stomach, panting, drooling, drinking and bringing the water back up immediately, and he may exhibit one or all of these symptoms. Bloat or distension is caused by a rapid build-up of gas in the stomach, which causes the stomach to distend and puts considerable pressure on the surrounding organs, so that the hound may go into shock. It is extremely painful and distressing for the hound, and is unmistakable, so that even a novice owner will be able to make a diagnosis. Often the stomach twists, (torsion), so that the entrance from the throat and the exit into the small intestine is cut off so that the gas has no means of escape and builds up even more rapidly. If the condition is not rectified immediately, the blood supply to the twisted areas is cut off and the tissue begins to die, causing necrosis.

There are different ways of treating the condition. Some vets will begin with a stomach tube, pushed down the throat and into the stomach which, with gentle palpation, may release some of the gas and make the patient more comfortable. (This is obviously not an option where the stomach has already twisted). Some vets will puncture the stomach through the side of the hound with a sterile hollow needle, which again releases the gas and eases the pressure. It is possible for anyone to be able to release the gas by the needle method. If you think you might want to use this method yourself, (and it would take considerable nerve to do this to your own dog, even in an emergency), then please find out the right way to go about it now, and obtain the necessary equipment from your vet. It is too late when it has actually happened. The gas needs to be released gradually as a sudden reduction in pressure would be too much of a shock to the system. Both these procedures are usually an interim measure to make the hound more comfortable and to ease the pressure on the abdomen before operating. Operations are usually successful in themselves but the hound will often die from shock, or after the operation from general trauma and from the toxins that build up in the system when the organs are damaged by inadequate blood supply and are unable to perform their natural functions. It is now usual for vets to tack the stomach to the body wall. This appears to help prevent bloat recurring, which used to happen all too often, and if it does recur the stomach is unable to twist.

Although there has been much research into bloat, the causes are still uncertain. However there may be a number of contributing factors:

1. Breed size, with the larger breeds more likely to get it. It is the size of the breed as a whole that matters, and a small Deerhound is as likely to get it as a large Deerhound.
2. Dogs with deep, narrow chests are more at risk. Here it is the individual that matters and the deeper and narrower the chest, the greater the risk.
3. Fast eaters are more at risk than slow, fussy eaters.
4. The fewer the number of meals per day, the greater the risk.
5. Eating a bigger meal than he is used to eating.
6. Personality - nervous and aggressive dogs are more at risk than happy, relaxed dogs.
7. Dogs with a history of belching or flatulence.
8. Time of day, with over half the number of cases occurring between 6 p.m. and midnight.

It does not seem to matter what sort of food the dog is fed, or whether the food is dry or soaked. Nor does it appear to matter how the dog is exercised in relation to feeding. Most dogs bloat when they are resting or sleeping.

One of the best pieces of advice I have seen about bloat was never to go home in the evening with an empty petrol tank, planning to fill it in the morning. If your Deerhound bloats overnight, you haven't the time to drive around looking for a petrol-station.

Eating unsuitable things
If you see your Deerhound eating something potentially dangerous, or if you are fairly certain that he has, seek advice as soon as possible from your vet. The remedy is not always to make the dog vomit - sometimes this can do more harm than good - but if this is

the advice given, it is possible to make him vomit by pushing a small amount of washing soda (about the size of a ten pence piece) down the throat, which will usually produce the offending substance fairly quickly. If this is not possible but you know for sure he has eaten something poisonous, then advice should be sought immediately from your vet or the nearest poisons unit. If you just suspect that he may have, seek advice to be on the safe side and observe very carefully for the next twenty-four hours.

Vomiting

There are times when it is natural for your hound to be sick, such as after eating grass. It is not that dogs are sick because they have eaten grass on a whim, but rather that they seem to use this as a natural emetic and eat it when they already feel the need to be sick. Maybe they have indigestion. It is not really necessary to stop them unless they are doing it excessively - in which case they may have an underlying problem - or if you have a white carpet.

Another time when it is perfectly natural is when a bitch regurgitates food for her puppies. This they will do from about seven weeks onward, though mine are more inclined to do it around ten or twelve weeks. It doesn't look very appetising when they do it in front of you or visitors, but the puppies certainly love it!

At other times they can vomit for no apparent reason after eating, then eat it up again and keep it down. Unless the hound seems off-colour, there is no problem.

Persistent vomiting, or accompanied by a temperature needs medical help. A mild bout of vomiting can sometimes be eased by a kaolin and morphine preparation. The hound should not be allowed to drink vast quantities of water, which will make him vomit again. It is better to remove the bowl and offer it to him frequently in small amounts, or leave a very little amount down in his bowl, renewed at intervals.

Excessive vomiting may cause the hound to become dehydrated, which can be seen if a fold of skin picked up on the withers stays folded rather than springing back to normal. Veterinary assistance is required, as re-hydration therapy may be needed. If it is impractical to get to a vet, then a home-made remedy can be given in the meantime. A pint of boiled and cooled water containing a tablespoon of glucose powder and a teaspoonful of salt can be given in small amounts until veterinary help is available.

Retching without bringing anything up can be a sign of something stuck in the throat, or may be the start of kennel cough.

The best indication of the severity of any condition like this is the behaviour of the hound. If he is distressed or uncomfortable, or 'just not himself', or if vomiting for no apparent reason is accompanied by drooling and/or stomach pain, the hound needs to be observed constantly in case anything more serious develops.

Diarrhoea

Many Deerhounds have slightly loose motions from time to time but it is very short-lived and they are otherwise normal. This is nothing to worry about and is usually caused by them having eaten something while out exercising.

If the hound has thin diarrhoea and an obvious stomach-upset, starve him for twenty-four hours and allow him only water in this time, nothing else, especially milk which will make the condition worse. If the diarrhoea subsides, re-introduce his food gradually in smaller amounts until you are sure he is back to normal.

Persistent diarrhoea needs veterinary advice, especially if it contains blood or is particularly evil-smelling. Re-hydration therapy may be needed (see previous section).

Kennel Cough

There is not always an obvious cough and sometimes the hound sounds more like he is retching. If you suspect your Deerhound may have this condition, isolate him, (although he will probably already have passed it to your other dogs in the incubation period), and seek veterinary advice, as antibiotics are sometimes required.

Do not take him anywhere, other than the vet's if necessary, (in which case leave him in the car and avoid the waiting room). Coughs are highly infectious and can be passed on via clothing and other things that the dog breathes on. He will not need his normal exercise which will exacerbate the cough, and the best thing to do is to keep him at a constant temperature indoors and away from other dogs.

Don't ever go to a show or anywhere where there are other dogs, even if you are a hundred per cent certain you are going to win that day! It is extremely selfish, and there is never any excuse for doing it. You may think your hound seems all right in himself but he may pass it on to others who will not cope so well. A bad dose of kennel cough can prove fatal in the very young or very old or infirm. Think how you would feel if you lost a dog you loved through someone else's selfishness.

Wounds

Superficial wounds can be bathed with a mild antiseptic solution and kept clean, which may mean cleaning each time the dog goes out. Occasional licking by the hound will keep the wound clean, but excessive licking should be discouraged as it will prevent the wound from skinning over. I find aserbine cream very effective in promoting the growth of new skin.

Wounds over two inches long or more than skin deep may need stitching, so a visit to the vet's will be necessary. If it does need stitching, try to persuade your vet to do it without a general anaesthetic, as anaesthetics are not without risk. Some will do it using a sedative and a local anaesthetic, depending, of course on the severity of the injury. After stitching, a plastic, Elizabethan-type collar may be needed to prevent the hound from removing the stitches, though mine tend to leave them alone once they have been told a couple of times.

Cysts

Some Deerhounds seem prone to getting sebaceous cysts, which usually remain quite small and almost unnoticeable. Occasionally, however, they can grow quite large and cause irritation to the hound. As long as they are causing no trouble, it is best to leave well alone. If they burst of their own accord or the hound scratches the top off, it will be necessary to clean out the area thoroughly and wash out with a mild antiseptic. If it becomes infected, then a course of antibiotics will be required.

If it is obviously causing discomfort, then veterinary advice is indicated. Cysts can be drained or removed, but that usually entails a general anaesthetic. They frequently recur.

Inter-digital cysts

These are reasonably common in older hounds, and will not go unnoticed because the hound will be lame. They are quite easily treated by soaking or bathing a few times a day in a solution of Epsom salts, which will ease the discomfort and promote healing. If it persists, or becomes infected, a course of antibiotics may be necessary.

Lameness

The answer to the question of lameness is rest. Usually the hound will make it obvious which leg he is lame on by taking his weight off it when standing, but a slight lameness is harder to detect. At the trot, if lame on a foreleg, he will take his weight off the sore leg and his head will nod as the sound leg hits the ground. If in a hind leg, the sound leg will be diagonally opposite the foreleg he nods on.

Once you have ascertained which leg is giving him the trouble, squeeze methodically from shoulder to foot, until he makes it obvious where it hurts. Cuts are easiest to deal with and should be bathed and assessed to see if they need stitching. If not, bathe twice a day with a warm antiseptic solution to keep clean.

Strains require more painstaking care if they are to get better quickly. The only answer is rest, which is more difficult in a young or very active hound but is not impossible, whatever some owners say. Patience is the only way to a quick recovery! Even a short run too soon will undo any healing that has already taken place. Total rest to start with, followed by lead exercise for a few days until you are certain that he is sound again should do the trick.

Broken or knocked-up toes

These are caused in a variety of ways and can occur in both good feet and bad. Unless there is other cause for concern, the best treatment is rest. The bone will eventually heal and the hound will be sound though, if actually knocked up out of place, the toe may look unsightly.

In a puppy, taping or bandaging the toe or foot will lead to undue weight being placed on the opposite sound leg, often resulting in a deformity in this leg rather than the injured one. The bandage would need to be changed daily as the puppy is growing so fast. For this reason, the foot should never be set in plaster of paris, which cannot be changed often enough and can result in serious deformity.

I have seen a case of toe which was removed on a front foot on a young male hound. This resulted in the rest of the foot becoming flat and long, as the remaining structure could not cope with the considerable weight of the hound, a greater percentage of which is on the forehand.

Rest is the answer, and any exercise should be gentle and on an even surface so as not to knock the toe again while it is healing.

Bursae

These are large, soft swellings occurring most often on the elbows and hip bones. They are very unsightly but do not appear to cause the hound any discomfort. It is often supposed that they are caused by the hounds having insufficient bedding, or lying on concrete or other hard surfaces. However, I am more inclined to think it is the manner in which the hound lies down rather than what he is lying on. I have had elbow bursae on two males, who both tended to let go and flop when half-way down, rather than sliding down as most of them do. Those bursae lasted quite a while even though the hounds had ample soft bedding, and one of them also recurred later. I have recently had a bursa on a bitch puppy, over the hip bone, and she also was very clumsy in the way she sat down. This one lasted only a couple of weeks. In all three cases the hounds were around six months old.

It is best to leave well alone, as draining them does not seem to be a permanent solution and they usually recur. In most cases they will go of their own accord.

Bleeding tail

Deerhounds, and any other breeds with long, thin tails, are rather prone to splitting the ends of their tails when wagging them or otherwise hitting them against hard surfaces. An owner can be horrified to enter a room liberally splattered with blood up the walls and on every surface if the hound has split his tail while playing. Unfortunately tails are one of the most difficult things to persuade to heal as there is no spare skin to stitch and not much blood supply to the end of it to promote healing, (although it didn't seem like it when you were cleaning the room!).

Prevention is better than cure and if you have the sort of hound that lashes his tail hard when greeting you or waiting for his food, for example, try to place him in a position where the tail will not catch on anything. It is the repetitive bashing that causes the trouble. As soon as you notice that the tail is bald at the end, it is time to change his habits to prevent it getting any worse as once it has split it will take much longer.

Once split, a tail must be protected in some way to enable it to heal. A light bandage will help but the shape of the tail means that it is difficult to get it to stay on so it must be securely taped on to the coat. Some people tape a plastic hair roller over the end to protect it. If the split isn't too bad, then once it is clean and dry, a coating of plastic skin may be enough. If bandaged, make sure the hound cannot remove the bandage. If the tail is badly split or really raw, it will be necessary to seek veterinary treatment, and in chronic cases, where the tail will not heal, it may be necessary to amputate the last two vertebrae in order to have some spare skin to stitch over the end.

Bald tail

Some puppies develop a bald patch on their tail, about half-way down. There is a gland at this point, which may contribute to the condition, and it is not helped by other puppies hanging on when playing. It is nothing to worry about and the hair will grow back eventually.

Prostate Glands

Some males, from around the age of five, may have trouble with their prostate gland, which swells and causes pressure on the rectum. The usual symptoms are one or more of the following - incontinence, with or without blood, straining to pass faeces that are narrower than normal, because of the constriction, or taking longer than usual to pass urine.

The causes can be infection, hormonal or a tumour. The hound will need veterinary treatment, which may be antibiotics initially or hormone treatment. If the latter is effective, one of the options is to castrate the hound to prevent it recurring. If neither of these treatments is effective, the possibility of a tumour should be investigated.

Bone Cancer

Deerhounds do not seem as prone to this as their heavier cousins, but there are a number of cases every year so it is worth a mention. It is usually, though not always, in the limbs and so the first sign is usually lameness without an apparent cause. If you have a number of hounds, then you will know there are often occasions where they knock themselves or pull muscles, in which case a few days' rest solves the problem. Bone cancer can sometimes display the same symptoms initially. If you are reasonably observant, and can tell on which leg the hound is lame, then checking the leg gently by squeezing methodically from top to bottom should indicate the problem area. At first there may be no discernible lump and a few days' rest may produce a recovery, as if it were a strain. The recurrence of the lameness may suggest that the hound has been less than careful and pulled the same muscle again. However repetitive lameness without obvious cause, marked tenderness in a joint or the subsequent emergence of a swelling, should be checked out by an x-ray. The swellings can be either along the length of the bone or at the joints, the latter being the more usual.

It is a more distressing illness than most as, at present, there is no cure and the disease progresses fairly rapidly. On the positive side, the owner has time to adjust to losing their companion and is able to make the hound's last weeks as pleasant as possible. On the down side, it involves the owner in making a very painful decision.

It is the worst part of owning a dog - the knowledge that you alone have the responsibility of deciding when the time has come to have him put down to save any further suffering. But it is a very important part of owning him, and should not be avoided or delayed unduly. It is the last kindness you can do for him and, when he is suffering, one of the most important of his life. Most owners can tell when the day has come, but in a condition that is terminal and getting worse each day, then it is better to put the dog down a day too early than a day too late. Bone cancer is usually a very painful condition and, although the hound will no doubt be on painkillers to make his life easier, it is the quality of life that is most important. It is most unfair to keep a dog alive if he is suffering simply because you haven't the moral courage to relieve his misery. If it can be arranged, euthanasia at home, on his own bed, with his owner giving him a cuddle is by far the kindest way to go, rather than at the vet's.

Some vets may offer to amputate the leg in order to extend the life of the dog. I do question the wisdom of this in Deerhounds, who are tall running hounds, and who sometimes seem to have trouble managing their legs when there are four of them. If this operation is contemplated, the owner must make sure that there are no secondary cancers, as is often the case, and make sure that they are not doing it for themselves, because they can't face life without the dog. In humans, it is possible to explain to them why they have lost a leg, but it must be traumatic for an animal to wake up to the pain and readjustment necessary, especially if chemotherapy is also required, which is unpleasant and would make the hound feel ill as well as having to cope with three legs. A young dog may have more resilience, but I would think it unkind to put an old dog through such trauma when he could end his life peacefully. However I believe there are cases where hounds have come through the operation well, though I don't know the age of the hounds concerned.

False Pregnancy

All bitches go through the same hormonal changes after a season, whether pregnant or not. With most the only signs are a slight disinterest in food between the third and fifth week after ovulation, and they are usually a little quieter until after the time they would have whelped. It is rare for a Deerhound bitch to have a bad false pregnancy, make beds and produce milk, but if your bitch really suffers, the only cure is to have her spayed. After a season bitches will not perform as well coursing or racing and it may be kinder to rest them.

Pyometra

This is an accumulation of pus in the uterus, usually occurring six to twelve weeks after a bitch has been in season. There are two types of pyometra. In the open type there is a thick, smelly discharge, of any colour from cream to reddish-brown from the vulva, and this type sometimes responds to antibiotics. The other type is a closed pyometra, which is not so obvious and is much more serious. It invariably requires an urgent operation or the bitch will become seriously ill.

The first sign of either is excessive drinking and the bitch will look poorly and have a temperature. They usually occur in bitches who haven't had a litter, but I have also known them in Deerhounds who have had puppies.

If you suspect that your bitch has a pyo, it is imperative to get to the vet without delay.

Portosystemic shunt (liver shunt)

This is a distressing condition acquired congenitally, or later in life due to disease, which causes the blood from the intestines to by-pass the liver and go back into general circulation, taking with it waste products and toxins which should be filtered out by the liver.

In the former, the liver has an inadequate blood supply and fails to develop normally, and the body is affected, to a greater or lesser degree, dependent on the severity of the shunt, by the waste products circulating in the body. Most shunts are detectable early in life, which is why it is important to have all puppies screened at around seven or eight weeks of age.

Early signs of the disease are excessive drinking and urine production, the urine abnormally dark or strong smelling; a tendency to loose stools; and a weakness or lack of co-ordination in movement, especially hind movement.

Later signs include stunted growth or poor condition, depression, lethargy, anorexia, nausea, ataxia, behavioural changes, stupor, aimless wandering, drooling, apparent blindness, kidney stones and intolerance to drugs.

Now that it is possible to test puppies, it should be less likely that anyone will have a Deerhound that is suffering from this condition, which is upsetting for both hound and owner. If your puppy has not been screened and there is suspicion that he may be suffering from this, there are a number of diagnostic tests that can be done to confirm it. The prognosis is poor.

Worms

After puppyhood, your Deerhound should be wormed every six months, or more often if you have young children or you suspect your hound has worms. Always buy the worming preparation from the vet and not from a pet-shop.

Round worms are the most common and are the sort that look like spaghetti. All puppies have them and are infected from the mother during pregnancy. Round worms are the ones with the bad press as the eggs, if ingested by humans, can hatch into larvae which migrate around the body. In most cases this causes no problem, but on rare occasions larvae enter sensitive tissue such as the eye. As long as children are discouraged from putting their fingers in their mouth when handling puppies and if all faeces are picked up completely, every day, there should not be a problem.

Tape worms are rarely seen in their entirety but segments are sometimes shed, which look like long flat seeds, or grains of rice. They need an intermediate host, the flea, to complete their life-cycle, and flea larvae swallow eggs shed by dogs, which remain in the flea until adulthood, and re-infect a dog who happens to kill and eat the flea. The eggs can also remain in pasture and can be ingested by cattle or other animals when grazing. The dog may then get tapeworms by eating raw or semi-cooked meat or parts of dead rabbits when out exercising. These days most worm preparations cover tape worms and various other types of worms that, though uncommon, are sometimes found in Britain, such as hookworms.

The most recent veterinary suggestions are that dogs should be wormed every six months, and that bitches should be wormed during each season, followed by another worming five weeks later, (i.e. approximately four times a year), as hormonal changes in the bitch at this time cause extra worm activity and this is a good time to attack the worms.

Fleas

Fleas can be the bane of a dog's life, and it may be necessary to spray him from time to time during the summer, which he will hate. Personally, I don't like to use any chemicals on my Deerhounds and prefer to spray the house instead, the theory being that this destroys their breeding grounds and is a better way of preventing the problem.

New products are coming onto the market all the time and it is now possible to feed your dog with a systemic insecticide which will kill the flea when it bites into the dog, or drops that are put on one part of the coat but protect the whole dog.

Flea collars can sometimes cause allergies and can be dangerous if the hound gets it caught on something while playing.

Ticks

Tick larvae are common in some areas and when they first land on the hound, from the blade of grass where they have been lying in wait, they resemble flattish triangular seeds, the point of which is embedded in the skin, very often around the eyes or ears. After becoming engorged on blood they look more like a greyish-brown pea.

They are very hard to dislodge from their host and there are many methods of loosening them. Placing a pad firmly over them is supposed to make them let go because they can't breathe. Also supposedly effective methods are holding a lighted cigarette end against them or soaking them in surgical spirit. Most people seem to just pull them out using their finger nails, (nail-biters would just squash them, of course), but if the head is left behind it may cause an infection. A friend told me recently that if you twist them clockwise they come out easily! (I wonder if it is anti-clockwise in the southern hemisphere ?) It is also possible to buy special tick tweezers, though I don't know how easy they are to use. You can leave the ticks to drop off by themselves but they tend to leave behind a bald patch around the area they have been sucking.

I am lucky to live in an area where ticks are not a problem, so I will have to leave you to try out these methods yourselves.

Blood pressure monitoring

This is a fairly recent thing and is undertaken by Angela Bodey. It came into being when it was discovered that many sight-hounds, and in particular Deerhounds, have high blood pressure when compared to other breeds. The procedure is aimed at showing whether high blood pressure causes other abnormalities or whether it is perfectly normal for this breed.

Blood pressure is measured by placing a cuff round the hound's tail and taking about ten readings. The heart is also listened to. This is all that is done in puppies. The adults also have a heart scan and an E.C.G., and have their eyes checked, as some abnormalities are apparent when examining the eyes.

It is possible by these methods to determine if there are any heart abnormalities, either congenital or acquired, and whether there are any rhythm disturbances such as atrial fibrilation.

Hundreds of Deerhounds have already been tested, but as much information as possible is needed in order to present a balanced picture.

Breedshow 1988 Newmarket

Breedshow 1985 Church Stretton

USEFUL ADDRESSES

The Deerhound Club:
Mrs S.M. Piggott
Woodleigh
Ghyll Road
Crowborough
East Sussex
TN6 1SU
Tel. 01892 662842

The Kennel Club
1 - 5 Clarges Street
London
W1Y 8AB
Tel. 0171 493 6651